OLD BRAND NEW

OLD BRAND NEW

COLOURFUL HOMES FOR MAXIMAL LIVING

Hardie Grant
BOOKS

DABITO

INTRODUCTION

Throughout my life, colour has served as my constant comfort, and creativity has always been my way of expressing how I feel. And although my career is now rooted in helping others transform their spaces, I lived twenty-six years before having a space that was all my own.

I was raised in a very small house in San Gabriel Valley, a suburb of Los Angeles, California, with a large Asian and Latinx immigrant community. I shared a bedroom with my mom, dad, and sister. My grandparents, aunts, and uncles shared the other two bedrooms and the garage. Living with nine people under one small roof sparked a curiosity in me about layout and organization. From the age of thirteen, I constantly wondered, *How can we save space, keep things tidy, and improve functionality and flow of movement?* So, I began to test my ideas. Whenever my mom was out of the house, I took the opportunity to rearrange the furniture: the beds in our bedroom went from an awkward L-shape to parallel. In the living room, I moved the couch around to improve the flow, and I added a desk for myself to create a more multifunctional space. I'd chip away at mountains of family members' belongings that seemed to pile up over the week and find clever places to stash things. In some ways I felt trapped in the circumstances of my improvised home, and these were the little things I could do to take ownership of my environment.

Without a space to call my own, I took shelter in exploring colour at the same time through art—it was an escape for me and an outlet for self-expression. My love for colour started at a very young age. As a kid I was obsessed with Lisa Frank's school supplies. Those vibrant, saturated, ombré colours were so outrageously beautiful and mesmerising. But nothing brought me more joy than Sanrio, the Japanese brand made up of colourful characters like Keroppi and the famous Hello Kitty. Ahiru No Pekkle was my favourite. From fourth to seventh grade, I participated in many Sanrio-sponsored colouring contests, and I won most of them. Even though I was a shy kid, I was fiercely competitive (I'm an Aries through and through).

Not only did I love colouring, but I was also good at drawing. In sixth grade I drew a bird-of-paradise flower on the cover of my journal because I admired its sculptural shape and the bold combination of orange, yellow, and green with a hint of purple. This is one of my earliest memories of my love for colour, and these colours continue to influence my work to this day.

In junior high school, I hit a rough patch. I was bullied. I was called *faggot*. Even though I had no idea what that word meant, I understood the shame that the slur was meant to impart on me—and it

Two influential figures in my life—my mom and aunt Holly in San Francisco in 1980.

affected me deeply. I didn't feel comfortable talking about this at home, so I had no safe space where I could express my feelings. But one day that all changed. An IKEA catalogue addressed to my aunt Holly arrived in the mail. When I opened the catalogue and flipped through the pages, I saw colourful, clean rooms full of happy people. I fantasised about making ramen in their Swedish-style kitchens. This catalogue became my bible. I flipped through it daily, ritually. This routine helped me pacify all my negative feelings and experiences. In some way, that was where I found my safe space. And that's where my initial love for interiors was sparked.

By my senior year of high school, I was done sleeping in the same room with my parents and sister, so I moved out on my own . . . to the living room. By then, I had accumulated three years' worth of styling inspiration, and I was finally ready to create a safe space of my own.

I went outside to our front yard and clipped snake plants, putting them in vases to decorate my living room–bedroom. Just a few plants instantly made the room warmer and calmer. Even back then, I understood the healing energy that plants could add to a space. I also began to experiment with taking my love for colour and infusing it into my surroundings. I begged my aunt Holly to take me to IKEA to get patterned yellow curtains to update the living room. Touring the showroom for the first time was mind-blowing. I did not know that every well-worn page I'd obsessed over and studied would be right there before me. Walking through each of the staged rooms in the store was better than Disneyland. Seeing these spaces in real life provided examples of what a home should look and feel like. It was monumental for me to realise that living in a beautiful place was within my reach. I still remember how amazing it felt to finally have some ownership in our shared home—the sight of those yellow curtains offered a daily improvement on my mood and sense of self.

This was my bedroom (that is, the family living room) growing up. I covered the sofa using a flat sheet to give it a new look. In the background are the patterned yellow curtains I asked my aunt Holly to buy for me, plus a glimpse of the snake plant in the corner. Next to me are my besties Anna and Han.

One of my lithographs from 2004.

I started college the following year at UC Santa Cruz. Go Banana Slugs! It was exhilarating to go somewhere new and leave my tight, shared quarters for a free-spirited place like Santa Cruz. I started off my studies as a chemical engineering major, but after a year I knew it wasn't for me. I decided to take a few intro-to-art courses, and this was when I fell in love

Very early vignettes I created right out of college. I've always loved a cluster of art and inspirations on a wall.

I gave this brown pot I found at a thrift store a yellow drip-paint update. Yellow has always been a major player in my style.

My sweet Beatrice and a DIY painted pouf.

with printmaking and photography. I had found my calling. I was finally able to channel everything I felt into my art. This was therapeutic for me after years of holding in my feelings. As a shy introvert, I found that experimenting with bold colours was exciting. Learning to mix inks also helped me to understand how different shades and hues played off each other (or didn't). It was more obvious than ever to me that colour was my thing.

During college, I was glued to the interior design makeover show *Trading Spaces*. My favourite designer was Vern Yip. It was my first time seeing someone who looked like me on TV doing something creative, and it helped me to imagine a creative career for myself. Soaking up the Swedish modernism from my beloved catalogue pages, the approachable designs shown on *Trading Spaces*, and the bohemian spirit of Santa Cruz, I began to explore my own decor style in my dorm rooms. I drew murals in them, hung art that I made myself, and draped orange sheets from the ceiling to create a faux canopy. I was thrifting, repurposing, and having fun with my space. And it was liberating.

After I graduated, I didn't know what I wanted to do, but I knew I wanted to travel and see the world. When a friend of mine became a flight attendant, I decided to apply for a job there as well. I didn't think I was going to get the job, but I did, and suddenly I was flying internationally several times a month. I traveled to Thailand, Taiwan, China, Hong Kong, Sydney, Paris, and back. I was inspired by wandering the streets in different countries and seeing how they used colour in creative ways.

When I wasn't flying around the world, I lived with my now-ex-heartmate in a downtown Los Angeles loft, and I got *really* serious about decor. This was the year I had four—four!—different sofas. I was a vintage vulture. Craigslist was essentially my design community.

I moved frequently. I explored different parts of LA and even lived in NYC briefly. Each rental had its own quirks and challenges, and I treated each one like a new client that I had to please. In 2010, I was inspired by blogs like *Design*Sponge* and *Apartment Therapy*. With my background in photography and graphic design, I thought I might give blogging a try, so I started to document my art, thrifting, and decorating adventures online. I called my blog *Old Brand New*. The name came to me one day because I wanted to write about how you can take old or vintage things and give them a new life or transform a space to take it from *old* to *new*. And the word *brand* represents you, your story, your identity, your experiences, your style. You put these three words together and it's all about the new touch, the new idea, the new floor plan. It's the revealing of yourself.

Through blogging I found not only a new passion but also a creative community and a new job as a graphic designer at a gardening company. I finally felt like I was on the right path. I grew my blog little by little and was thrilled when my work began appearing in publications like *ELLE Decor*.

Throughout the years, I honed my styling game and photography skills to capture interiors. I don't believe you need to be a formally trained designer to have a beautiful or stylish home. Or even be a trained photographer to take a great photo of your space. We can all tap into our creative selves to make our homes feel special. If someone like me can do it, then I believe anyone else can do it, too.

BEFORE

This shotgun home in New Orleans was the first makeover I created for someone other than myself. It made me realise how meaningful it was and how much I loved the process of transforming a space.

HOW TO USE THIS BOOK

I am going to show you spaces that are relatable to everyone, including rentals or homes with absolutely zero existing architectural details. You can transform your home into something unique, colourful, and beautiful—from drab to Dab! I want my story to serve as a testament that you can create a place where you can fully and safely express who you are. Whether you own, rent, or share a small space with three generations, your home can be a celebration of *you*.

This book invites you into over fifty rooms that I have designed, styled, and photographed over the course of my career. Each page reveals meaningful makeovers—spaces I helped to "Dabify" for my family, friends, and clients. You'll find a section in each chapter called "What Would Dab Do?" that will walk you through my process of designing a room.

Each chapter of this book starts with the **OLD**. What history, habits, or old ways of living need to change for the inhabitants of each space? How about the old bones of the home? The architectural details? The existing furniture and accessories? What are the old aspects of the home that need to change? What needs to be preserved?

Next, we'll dig into the **BRAND**. What is the story or style of the people who currently live in the home? What makes them tick? What colours move them? Where are they from? What parts of them will be expressed in their space?

Then, we'll move on to the **NEW**. What's the plan? What new vibes will we invite into the space? How will we Dabify the home to make it more beautiful, more functional, but most of all, more *them*?

I'll take you on a journey to see my personal spaces, as well as the homes of family, friends, and clients in between. This will show you how I design my space and how I design for others. We'll start with my current LA home and end with my new New Orleans home.

Also included in this book are styling tips I've learned along the way to help you get your space magazine ready. I'm also sharing some fun DIY projects you can try out in your own space. Let's bring in some colour and pattern!

By the end of this book, it is my hope that you'll feel inspired to own your space and maximise your style. I hope you will begin to build your colour confidence and make your home as vibrant as your personality. You deserve a beautiful space to come home to. More importantly, you deserve a safe space, a place to foster healing energy and creativity, one that allows you to protect, value, and express yourself.

So, let's decorate and celebrate all the intangible experiences and tangible objects you've collected throughout your life, and learn to pull it all together to turn something Old into something Brand New.

I WANT THIS BOOK TO EMPOWER YOU TO TAKE OWNERSHIP OVER YOUR SPACE— WHETHER YOU OWN OR RENT.

Paper

Familia feliz

SURF
THROUGH
LIFE

CASS

MY PROCESS: WHAT WOULD DAB DO?

I believe that overthinking stifles creativity. With so many choices out there when it comes to design, people end up feeling overwhelmed by all the different approaches they could take to decorate their space that they end up not doing anything. But simply trying something out—even if it doesn't work in the end—is a necessary step in figuring out what will be right for your home. It's like trying on different sizes of clothes. It's like dating. You don't know until you try, right? So, try painting one wall a different colour, or try a piece of furniture, like an armchair in yellow, to see if you like it. Maybe it'll inspire you to get a sofa that's orange next time as you build your colour confidence.

Some of that initial overthinking usually has to do with design styles. Everyone seems to want to know what their interior design style is these days, but I think we get too caught up on singular style and categorizations. And my own style . . . is it traditional? Modern? Farmhouse? Bohemian? Industrial? Victorian? 1970s? Art deco? Well, it's all of that and more! It's eclectic, eccentric, and maximal. It's all about mixing styles, and that's what makes design sing. Let's focus on colours, memories, culture, heirlooms, shapes, and materials. Pay attention to the hues, patterns, feelings, and textures you like, and your own unique style will follow. So much of design is evoking a feeling in a space. If you tap into the things that make you feel happy, safe, motivated, and inspired—and put those things into your home—it will result in a style that is all you.

Design is also about working with what you've got. Sometimes, that could mean a ceramic vase from Target or a vintage Thonet bentwood chair from Goodwill. It could mean painting an old planter to give it new life. It's all about finding a balance in mixing old and new.

Over the years I got my own overthinking out of the way. Eventually my design process fell into place. Now I have a plan of attack each time I go to design a room, and that makes designing a space much less daunting. Let's break my process into seven easy steps to help you figure out what your space needs while asking, "What would Dab do?"

1

STEP 1

LET YOUR SPACE SERVE YOU ——— DISCOVER YOUR MUST-HAVES

Think about what you need in your space. What's not working? How can the items you already have better serve you? Do you need to rearrange? Do you need more storage? How do you use this space every day? Is your space multifunctional? How is the lighting? Ask yourself what your must-haves are. Once you figure out all the pieces, you will have a better understanding of what you can fit in the space as you plan and shop.

This living room is from our New Orleans home (see chapter 10, page 233). I was playing around with paint colours. Sometimes you need to paint two walls to realise that you only need one accent wall.

STEP 2

FIND YOUR FLOW ———
CREATE YOUR FLOOR PLAN

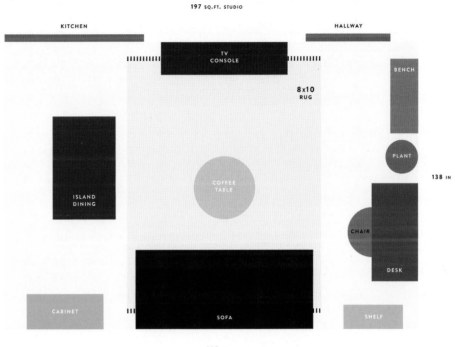

197 SQ.FT. STUDIO

KITCHEN · HALLWAY

TV CONSOLE

8x10 RUG

BENCH

PLANT

138 IN

ISLAND DINING

COFFEE TABLE

CHAIR

DESK

CABINET

SOFA

SHELF

205 IN

Next, we find our flow. To do this, I first measure the space—the walls, hallways, doors, windows, and fireplaces that could affect the layout. Then I create a simple Photoshop document of the floor plan I'm envisioning for the room (you can easily do this with graph paper and a pencil, too). Depending on the room and how big the space is, there are certain things I always like to keep in mind—and they begin with where you place your furniture and your rug size.

Furniture and rug placement will provide the foundation you need to cement your floor plan. Being mindful of how you need to move around and flow in and out of your space will help you make decisions about your furniture and how far apart it needs to be from other items in the room. For example, in a living room, I like to have at least 15 to 20 inches of clearance between a sofa and a coffee table. If it's a path that will see a lot of foot traffic, I like to leave a minimom of 24 inches of space. For rugs, the bigger the better—the trick is to fill up the space! A larger rug will ground the room and make it feel more defined and balanced. For example, if you put a 4 by 6-foot rug in a 9 by 12-foot room, the rug will look tiny and make the room feel unbalanced. Instead, using an 8 by 10-foot rug for that 9 by 12-foot room will define the space and make it seem larger overall.

Once your floor plan is complete, you may still need to try out different configurations of your furniture just to see how it feels. Sometimes the layout you had planned in your head doesn't work out in real life. You'd be amazed at how a simple layout change can alter the flow and increase the quality of your life.

STEP 3

COLOUR STORY ———
UNCOVER YOUR COLOURS

Now the fun part begins! Let's uncover your colours. Pull inspiration from your wardrobe, a favourite rug, a nostalgic piece of art, your favourite plant, a memorable trip, or something or someone meaningful to you that will help you home in on colours that light you up and bring you joy. Spend some time identifying hues that give you good vibes and make a positive impact on your mood. Write down these colours in a notebook or even make a mood board of them.

Once you've unearthed your colours, think about how they will balance one another. I like to balance warm and cool colours. If I choose a coral colour, for example, I might pair it with Kelly green. If you work with a mustard colour, you might find a teal blue to go along with it. I also like to work

with two warm colours, like you see in this photo of the French Quarter in New Orleans. The mustard and coral tones inspired the bedroom you see on the left. Once you have your two dominant colours, then you can sprinkle in accent colours to your heart's content. And don't be shy about it! Don't worry too much about your colour combinations. Colours have a way of vibing together. Just think about which colours make you feel good!

Now that we've identified our colour palette, let's make these colours twerk! It's all about the balance. If your rust-coloured velvet statement sofa is the protagonist of the room, the peaches-and-cream wall colour should play the supporting role. If you go wild with a tropical wallpaper, you may want to extract a solid colour from the wallpaper for your furniture.

STEP 4

SOURCE AND STYLE ———
SHOP TILL YOU DROP

Left: Mate Gallery in Montecito, California. Right: L'Atelier 55 in Paris, France.

I love to shop at flea markets and antique shops to source one-of-a-kind pieces and see, feel, and learn about the different styles and eras those pieces are from. If there aren't any nearby or you prefer to source online, online marketplaces like Chairish, Etsy, eBay, and Facebook are a few places where you can find real treasures. Oftentimes the sellers share a bit of history about the pieces, and through the product listings you can learn new keywords and uncover similar pieces in that style. For example, when I first started decorating, I had no idea what chinoiserie or chintz was. But in combing through online marketplaces and googling the term, I began to learn that I loved pieces with a lot of pattern. Spending time looking through these online marketplaces helped me figure out what I liked and what that style was called so I could look for more pieces in the same vein.

Shipping can be costly for bigger pieces, but remember that you can always search for "local"

results. And don't hesitate to message the seller to negotiate. I do it all the time, and you'll be surprised how you can score a deal if you ask.

Another tip? I simply search for "sculptural" pieces. These pieces don't have to be vintage; they can be new as well. For example, I'll google "sculptural coffee tables or lighting." Put "sculptural" in front of anything you're searching for. That's usually how I hunt for statement pieces and find some real gems that will lend depth to my design.

Before pulling the trigger on something, be sure to cross-reference the items with your floor plan. You have to be sure the dimensions of the item fit your space (and that you can get the item through the front door!). I once ordered a chandelier online, but when it arrived and I tried to hang it from the ceiling, I realised it was way too big—it came all the way down to my shoulders and would never work for my home. Whoops!

STEP 5

CREATE A MOOD BOARD ———
MOCK IT UP

I like to create mood boards as I shop. I take photos of items I find in real life and pin my online finds to Pinterest. It helps to see things grouped together to get a sense of how the items will play off each other in a room. Once I have sourced all the items for a space, I also like to create a separate Photoshop document like the one above. It's amazing how accurate it is when everything comes together in real life. If Photoshop isn't your jam, then print

out the images and move them around on a sheet of paper or a bulletin board. This will help you see how the room will come to life. There are also apps like Morpholio Board and Spoak to help you create mood boards. You can also sketch out your plan on a piece of paper—simply visualising your space before you get started is always helpful, and you don't have to be a master mood-boarder to do it.

STEP 6

YIN AND YANG ———
BRING ON THE BALANCE

Now that you're in the process of creating your space, think about the yin and yang, which is all about balance. Balance warm and cool colours, balance sharp and round shapes, balance light and dark, balance small and big, balance scale and proportions, balance old and new. When you keep this in mind, it's easier to create a layered and rich space. This will help to guide your design decisions.

Are there too many vintage things? Then let's find some new, contemporary pieces to balance it out. Is the space too hard? Find some natural materials and textures like cane or rattan to make it feel softer. Paint surfaces or add textiles. Are the walls too bare? Add more art. Is everything the same height? Add some taller pieces for variation. Remember that opposites do attract. Experiment with that tension.

STEP 7

FIND YOUR FOCAL POINT ——————
WOW IT OUT

Every space deserves that "wow" moment. As you design your space, identify what that moment is for you—what is the focal point? It could be a floor-to-ceiling gallery wall, an oversise piece of art, a striking wallpaper, a large indoor tree, graphic tiles, or maybe it's a gigantic window that invites in the greenery from outside. Those are the things that will make your space sing. You want to walk in and be wowed!

This room is asymmetrical. To help it feel more balanced, it's important to identify a focal point. The far wall is the only solid wall, and it's the first thing you see when you walk into the room. To make it a focal point, a large piece of framed art is hung above a bright cobalt sofa. The two pendant lamps further draw the eye in and help to frame the room.

DABITO'S LOS ANGELES HOME

OLD

After being a nomad for most of my life, I finally saved up enough money to buy my first home in Los Angeles. While I wasn't in love with the house straightaway, I saw its potential. My cookie-cutter home was built in 1952, and it had zero architectural details. All the rooms were basic boxes. The only attribute this house had at the time was that it was built on a hill with a partial view. The house was lightly renovated by flippers who, as with most quick flippers, did a janky job.

BRAND

Since this is my first home, I wanted the space to be an extension of me, my journey, and my personal style. This was the first time I could totally transform a space without worrying about landlords or clients. I wanted this house to remind me of the creative path I took to get here, as well as my favourite places, like Hong Kong, Thailand, and Mexico City. It was important for me to hang artworks I created throughout the years, making it my own personal art gallery. Because if you don't celebrate yourself, who will? I also wanted to infuse the house with all of my favourite colours, such as yellow, green, teal, terra-cotta, fuchsia, and cobalt blue.

NEW

My must-haves were a functional primary bedroom and en suite bathroom, the addition of a laundry room, and an overhaul of the other bathrooms, the kitchen, and backyard. After all, entertaining friends and family in this home is important to me and my husband, Ryan. I wanted my home to be a hub for gatherings and being together with my chosen family. Most importantly, I wanted to wow out those basic-ass boxes.

A STUDY IN CUSTOMISATION & APPRECIATION IN MY LA HOME

MONOCHROMATIC KITCHEN

We've established that I adore colour and how colours can transform a space, and that transformation can also go either way: good or bad. One of my least favourite colours, or shades, is grey. The original kitchen was less than fifty shades of grey and about as boring as can be. The backsplash had uneven grout lines, and the tile work was completely crooked, which drove me bananas.

The most important step in creating a design for your space is to think about the colour story. Since I have an open-concept floor plan, I wanted the kitchen to feel more defined. To achieve that, I went for a bold, monochromatic, tone-on-tone feel. For kitchens, I like drawing inspiration from my favourite foods. My favourite herb is a shiso, which is used in many Vietnamese, Japanese, and Korean dishes.

To balance the cool green tones in this space, I brought in a vintage Moroccan rug for accent that I found at the flea market. Its warm colours in yellow, peach, and orange remind me of nuóc măm (Vietnamese dipping sauce, pronounced "nook mom"). Remember that accent colours can be whatever you like. The artwork picks up similar colours in the rug and the wall colour, which helps tie the whole space together. A small table lamp can be a great and unexpected way to add more lighting into your kitchen.

One way to design your space is through tone-on-tone colour. Pick one colour and make it the star. Here, green is the star. Then you can choose accent colours like orange and yellow.

BEFORE

20

What used to be an empty space next to the fridge now houses custom upper and lower cabinets. To create a bit of interest and detail, and because it's such a tight space, the cabinets were intentionally rounded to allow a smooth flow into the kitchen from the dining room. This now serves as our favourite little bar area. We turned an unused space into an area full of life and functionality.

We replaced the entire wall of backsplash with only 5 inches of an emerald-green Moroccan tile. Tiles can be expensive, especially these handmade ones, so two rows of tiles were an affordable option. I used the same semi-gloss enamel cabinet paint on the walls since it's durable and easy to clean.

For a seamless look, we created a drywall box to conceal the hood and updated to a slide-in range, which is less bulky without the back controls—those knobs were totally ruining the kitchen vibe.

I love to entertain. We often have family and friends over for hot pot, mahjong, karaoke, and cocktails. The kitchen is an incredibly important, high-traffic, high-use space, which is why it needs to be beautiful and functional.

TIKI MODERN DINING ROOM

This small dining room was an open-concept space that lacked any style. It's not a big space, so it can truly only fit a small round dining table to allow an easy flow. My plan was to maximise the space with an eat-in nook, and add a banquette on both walls to create more seating. This configuration allowed us to graduate from a 48-inch round table to a 60-inch round table.

After refinishing the kitchen with a bold green, the dining room needed something equally striking to interact with it. Since the kitchen was painted a solid hue, I decided to use a patterned wallpaper to add depth and lushness. It's now the space I use the most—not only for eating, but I work, paint, and even take naps with my kitty, Verbena, here.

BEFORE

I love a variety of lighting options for a space, especially in a dining room. The chandelier didn't offer enough ambience, so a plug-in sconce along with a table lamp on a pedestal add a warm glow while also adding height and accents.

HOW COLOUR TELLS A STORY

If you have trouble picking out a colour, sometimes I recommend thinking about someone special in your life and what their favourite colour is. That can often be a sweet jumping-off point. Purple is one of my aunt Holly's favourite colours, so I decided to start with that story in the dining room.

The purple dining room sits directly across from the green kitchen, so I had to make sure the spaces were completely cohesive and didn't compete or clash with each other. Since the kitchen is so bold with its solid green colour, I brought in a beautiful tropical wallpaper pattern for the dining room that has hints of both purple and green in it. I chose a gorgeous black, sculptural round dining table to ground the space and hold its own without getting lost in all the colour. A green rug and pillows with hints of purple and peach unify both spaces.

If you have necklaces you no longer wear or are heirlooms, try hanging them on a lamp base for a playful touch.

ECLECTIC LIVING ROOM

COMING FULL CIRCLE

When I bought this house, I immediately knew I wanted to use the colour yellow for the living room. And there's no better way to create a living-room statement than choosing a sofa in the dominant colour you want to go with. This goes back to some of the origin stories I shared in the introduction, when I picked out circular-patterned yellow curtains for my living room–bedroom in high school. I couldn't help but think about how far I had come: not only did I have my own *separate* living room and bedroom, but in my very own house! To me, this was a meaningful full-(yellow)-circle moment. That's the vibe, history, and story I wanted to bring into this room.

We're big TV watchers, so I had to move the sofa around a few times to figure out the layout. Layout is so important because it helps create a flow in your space and, ultimately, your life. Your living room layout should welcome you in without feeling cumbersome or like you have to dance around objects to get into a comfortable position. We finally ended up with the TV across from the window. The Samsung Frame TV (on opposite page) looks like a piece of artwork when it's not being used. An art gallery wall around the TV disguises the screen when it's turned off.

THE MORE THE MERRIER

I think people are often afraid of filling a room with things because it might feel cramped, but I feel quite the contrary. The more you fill a space up, the more welcoming and cosy it becomes. For example, I love having a couple ottomans in my living room to add extra seating, colour, and pattern to the space.

WINDOW TREATMENTS

Here's a way to define your living room: try matching your Roman shades to the colour of your sofa. I chose yellow instead of green (which would have matched the dining room and kitchen) because that option ties in all the spaces together. The kitchen and dining room windows are both on the same side of the home, so they felt like they needed to be the same. But since the living room window is perpendicular and doesn't share the same wall with the others, it could be separate.

Roman shades are my favourite window treatments because they are easier to install and still feel very custom and finished. Curtains are trickier to use because it can be difficult to find the right sizes for your particular window dimensions and ceiling height combination.

An open-concept floor plan can be great for making a small house feel bigger, but it can also be tricky to define and tie in all the spaces. My trick is to sprinkle in accent colours that are in nearby spaces to unify. For example, in the living room I have a purple pouf and a green tabletop vase to reflect the dining room. And the kitchen has colours of purple and yellow to echo the colours from the living room. Now all the spaces feel unified and intentional.

A stack of books can also double as an accent table.

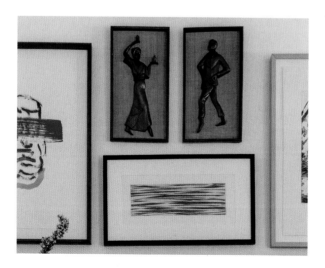

When creating a gallery wall, try mixing different types of frames and art, like this Filipino Tinikling dance wood-carved piece that is from my partner's mom, who bought it in the Philippines.

This large Ficus Audrey helps breathe life into the space. Over the years, I've learned to actually minimise my plant babies because as much as they add greenery and life into the space, they also require responsibilities, and that can sometimes weigh me down. And because a large plant has an established root system, it helps me keep it alive. But that's just me. If you can nurture twenty plants in a room, then by all means, you do you.

Large pots with a pretty design can be hard to come by, so I grabbed a piece of fabric and wrapped it around the planter. This piece of fabric is made of hemp from the Naga tribe, who live in northeastern India and Myanmar. I painted the piece of art behind the fabric-covered planter almost twenty years before I bought the fabric on Etsy. It just goes to show that when you lean into colours that you love, they will all magically and timelessly work together.

When I have creative blocks, I like to go through my travel photos. I find photos with beautiful colour combinations to use as a starting point. If I home in on one dominant colour, then these photos give me inspo for the accent colours. In this case, a photo from my travels to Peru inspired a room with a yellow sectional sofa, a pink lounge chair, and lush green plants.

FOLK ART OF THE AMERICAS

OS MOTA   BEIGE IS NOT A COLOR

LIGHT FIXTURES

Think of lights as the jewelry in your room. You want a dazzling earring hanging from the ceiling. I like to always have at least three different types of lights in a space to make it feel warm and intimate in the evening: a floor lamp, table lamp, and ceiling light. If you can add a sconce, that's a chef's kiss. Also consider adding dimmers—they make a world of difference and allow you to customise the brightness in your space. Incorporating varying light sources adds scale, ambience, and interest to a room.

BRIGHT & INVITING ENTRYWAY

The entryway is such an important part of the home, but it often gets overlooked as merely a passageway to the main living spaces. I want you to think of this as the very first impression of your home: the beginning of your story. The original entryway of my home was dark and had a solid door. I brightened things up by installing a glass front door that let in plenty of sunlight. A slim bench serves as a place to store a few pairs of shoes, mail, keys, and other bric-a-brac. Even though it's such a small space, I was able to create a very special entryway moment by hanging one of my favourite fiber pieces, which I found at a thrift store way back in 2010 for fifty dollars.

BEFORE

CURVY & COLOURFUL HALLWAY

Since this house was so plain with zero architectural details, it desperately needed interest and intrigue, and this hallway was the best place to add those. I hired a contractor to rip out the old laminate flooring and installed herringbone wood floors in a rich walnut colour to add dimension. An archway was added, lending a historical touch. Sometimes we need a splash of that old-world charm in a new space. Bifold doors for the hallway closets save space and add earthy texture. There used to be a solar tube in the hallway, but I didn't like the diffused light it gave off. I want to be able to look up and see the sky, so I swapped it out for a skylight, and it brings in the perfect natural-light quality I was looking for.

For wall colour, I chose terra-cotta, inspired by Mexican architect Luis Barragán. When I visited Barragán's studio in Mexico City, I was astounded by his specific colour choices and how he deliberately pairs colour and light to accentuate a space, in a manner similar to James Turrell. Throughout the day, the quality of light and colour changes, which I think is so poetic in marking time and the course of our daily cycles. Colour gives me energy—when I get out of bed and see a fiery terra-cotta in the hallway or the green or purple in the kitchen and dining room, it fuels me and wakes me up. And since I don't drink coffee, colour is my caffeine!

BEFORE

ASIAN-INSPIRED HOME OFFICE / GUEST ROOM

This room was a boring space with mirrored sliding doors on one side, so we Dabified it into a multifunctional office/library/lounge/guest room!

My main inspiration for this room was a print by Vietnamese French painter Mai Trung Thu. I found it at a vintage store in Los Angeles called The LuxeLust Life, and I gravitated toward the colours in the artwork. For this space, I wanted to celebrate my Vietnamese-Chinese roots and travels to Thailand and China. I sprinkled in some of my finds from Bangkok, such as the hand-carved elephant and vintage framed photos of beloved Thai King Bhúmibol Adulyadej and Queen Sirikit.

For the desk, I chose a built-in option that was custom-made by my friend at Alder & Oil. This floating desk now occupies the space where the mirrored closet used to be. A traditional palm wallpaper brings visual interest that is tropical, but also subtle, neutral, and calming. The wallpaper completely transformed the space and added a layer of richness and texture.

This multipurpose space now fosters both productivity and rest. For overnight guests, the sofa has a pull-out bed.

BEFORE

HIRE A PROFESSIONAL

I consider myself to be capable when it comes to wallpaper. I've installed removable wallpaper before, and it came out great, so I thought installing traditional wallpaper myself would be no problem. Boy, was I wrong. It requires a totally different skill set and technique. I'm gonna be real with you all: If you're super precise and patient, then this might be right up your alley, but for me, I found it challenging. Save yourself the time, tears, and hair pulling, and hire a pro to install it.

JADE JUNGLE BATHROOM

This bathroom started out with a mismatching combination of most likely leftover materials the old flippers pieced together to make it look presentable. The sink was tiny, and the bathtub was old.

Bathrooms are the best rooms to go bold with your design choices. The bathroom colour story is inspired by an acacia tree from my backyard, which led me to find these green cement tiles that have a similar graphic line quality to the acacia. I applied a bright white grout using $\frac{1}{16}$-inch grout lines, which added more lines and detail to the pattern. Different grout colours and grout widths can really change the look and feel of your space, so consider your choices.

I used 2 by 8-inch glossy white subway tiles installed in a herringbone pattern for the shower walls. Laying tiles in a herringbone pattern is a longer process because it requires more cuts and precision, and it can also add to the cost. The white grout makes the herringbone pattern appear less busy than a darker grout would.

Now, let's talk about the ledge that runs along the entire wall both in and outside of the shower. I got a deal on a prefabricated Calacatta Alaska quartz slab that was intended for a kitchen island. Having the slab run wall to wall visually elongates the bathroom. It adds more surface space for toiletries, but let's be real—it's really to hold more plants. Plants add life, greenery, and a relaxing vibe to a room. Especially if you have a small space, plants give the feeling of lushness or that you're bathing outside. In a room that typically has hard materials, plants add the balance of softness.

SEAL THE DEAL

Cement tiles require extra care during installation. If you're hiring a contractor to install cement tiles, make sure they are familiar with the process. I recommend always sealing the tiles before installation to protect them from stains, especially from grout. I have unfortunately seen black cement tiles that were not sealed properly before grouting, which left them looking hazy from the grey grout installation.

BEFORE

PITCH PERFECT

One thing I learned about bathroom renos is that it's all about the pitch. And I'm not talking about singing. The shower floors, niche, or the ledge all need a pitch so that water can easily roll down and into the drain. Water should not sit anywhere. This is where form follows function. If things don't function properly, it doesn't matter how beautiful it is. Or as my dad likes to say in Cantonese, "Looks good but doesn't taste good."

MODERN MEDITERRANEAN PRIMARY BEDROOM & EN SUITE BATHROOM

WHAT WOULD DAB DO?

DISCOVER YOUR MUST-HAVES

My home originally had four bedrooms and two bathrooms that were all on the smaller side. An important need for me was a bigger primary bedroom that could fit a king-size bed along with a bigger closet. I also wanted an en suite bathroom that had a walk-in shower with double shower heads, a double vanity, and an enclosed toilet room. This sounds like a tall order, and it took some Tetris maneuvering to figure out the best layout for us.

CREATE YOUR FLOOR PLAN

I was a bit reluctant about consolidating two rooms to create my dream space because I was worried about resale value. But at the end of the day, your home should reflect your lifestyle and how you want to live in it. Having an intentional space that I love and use every day outweighs having two neglected small spaces.

I proceeded to measure both spaces and sketched it out on Photoshop. It took a lot of figuring out how to utilise the space, and I came up with a plan that involved putting a wardrobe along one side of the wall. I asked my contractor to tell me all the minimom code requirements for a toilet room so I could figure out the best flow.

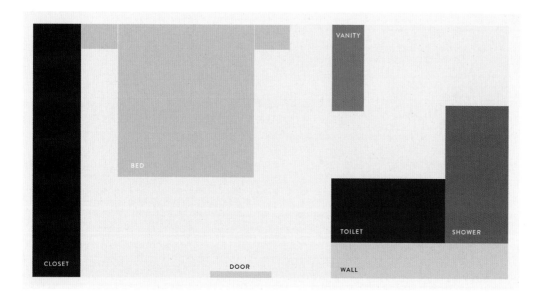

VANITY

BED

TOILET   SHOWER

CLOSET   DOOR   WALL

A great tip on splurging and saving: install the IKEA PAX wardrobe system and raise it so that it almost touches the ceiling. This almost looks like a fun accent wall instead of practical closets. The cane doors were custom-made, a splurge to elevate the wardrobe.

Since the floor-to-ceiling cane closet wall in the bedroom draws so much attention, I ended up adding the built-in shelving to the opposite wall to add interest to the other side of the room. In the bathroom, I repeated the wood tones from the bedroom. Wood, while being a hard material, feels like a softer element than tile and other stone materials because it has an earthiness to it. Since we have wood flooring and cane doors on the closet wall, I wanted the bathroom to echo those tones while softening all the tile in the space at the same time. This was also important because there is no door separating the rooms. Lastly, I balanced the design by bringing a patterned wallpaper into the toilet room. This was the perfect complement to all the solid paint and tile.

WOW IT OUT

I wanted multiple wow moments in both the bedroom and the bathroom, starting with the large window behind the bed. I know fêng shui discourages a window there, but with Roman shades pulled down at night, it's practically like a wall. We have a huge fig tree outside our window along with some bougainvillea, and it's so lush during late spring to early winter that I feel like I'm in a jungle in Bali. Opposite the cane wall are built-in shelves with an archway in the middle. This archway creates another wow moment before you step into the en suite bathroom. The walk-in shower also has an arch with Zellige tiles. These spaces are now jam-packed with personality.

STYLING BOOKCASES AND SHELVES

I created this built-in bookcase for the sole purpose of displaying my favourite souvenirs, artworks, and plants. When it comes to styling shelves, think of a zigzag. You want to arrange items with varying heights on each shelf, as well as from top shelf to bottom shelf, in order to create that zigzag effect to carry the eye around the shelves. Sometimes it can be hard to find a substantial piece to fill a shelf, and artworks are perfect for achieving that. Layer the shelves, have things overlap. Try placing objects or lamps in front of artworks. Group similar objects together. Alternate books, plants, and objects so they move in a diagonal line from top to bottom. Think of each shelf as a bookscape with a variety of heights.

For this bathroom, my inspiration came from Seville, Spain, which is where my husband's parents got engaged. The city was filled with terra-cotta arches and geometric tiling, so I brought some of that charm into the space.

SHOP TILL YOU DROP

For the double sink, it was nearly impossible to find one that measured 48 inches to place in a double vanity. Seeing what is out on the market and what sizes are available—whether in person or online—will help you figure out what is right for your own space. Don't get discouraged! It may take some scrolling until you find the right piece. Using the filter function on a retailer's website to specify size, colour, style, and so on will help you weed out the options that won't work for you. I eventually found and purchased a vanity base and put in a trough sink that would give us the double sink option.

In the shower, terrazzo floors from Concrete Collaborative add a subtle pattern. Terrazzo is a concrete material made up of bits of marble, granite, and glass chips. Because the wall tiles are solid, the flooring needed texture for balance. Pulling colours from the terrazzo floors and using them elsewhere in the space, like the Behr "Golden Aura" paint on the shower enclosure, helps define the space and accentuates the arched shower door.

54

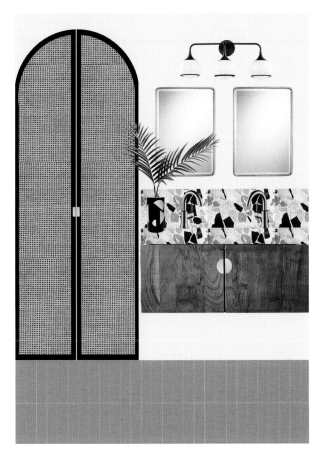

When I initially mocked up this bathroom, I had my heart set on a custom-made terrazzo sink. But after pricing out costs for that, I ended up going with a prefab sink that fit the budget and still looked great. Sometimes you have to design and troubleshoot as you go, but my mock-up was a great starting point for this room. Having a mock-up was also super helpful for my contractor and their team so we could all be on the same page about how I wanted this project to look in the end.

CHOOSING BATHROOM FIXTURES

Don't be afraid to mix different finishes like brass, champagne bronze, or gold with matte black and brushed gold finishes. For example, in this bathroom I used a champagne-bronze finish on the faucets and matte black light fixtures. You can mix up to three different metals in a space. I typically like to pair chrome or brushed nickel (metals that are often already at play in some existing spaces, like rentals) with brass and matte black lighting fixtures, plumbing fixtures, or cabinet hardware. As a general rule for mixing metals, there should be two dominant metals, and the third should be used very sparingly. Using the same finish throughout the room can also look cohesive, and you can't go wrong with that.

CINNAMON & MINT BATHROOM

This guest bathroom is standard size (about 5 by 8 feet). It had no windows, so it was completely dark. I always want natural light in all my spaces, and a skylight was the only option that instantly brightened up the space. I was inspired by my trip to Mexico City, where I found some colourful dice in orange and green, and decided that was my bathroom's colourway. I also wanted the floors to be green so they would be cohesive with the other two bathrooms I renovated in the house. Now, you don't have to do that; I wanted to be intentional about unifying the three bathrooms in the house. To create a wow moment in a small space, install floor-to-ceiling Zellige tiles. And here's a fun tip: you can make your shower glass doors curved to add a bit of unexpected detail. Ask your contractor or glass specialist about it.

BEFORE

TWO-TONED OFFICE

The colour story for my office was inspired by my trip to Kyoto, Japan. I loved the colour combination of bengara red and green copper roofs at the shrines. I attempted to use those colours in the space with Farrow & Ball "Eating Room Red" on the walls and "Arsenic" on the ceiling. A dining table is used as a desk to provide a larger workspace. I've always wanted a floating desk to maximise movement. It reminds me of art school. A Beni Ourain rug with green stripes, two cane closets, and purple bouclé ottoman all add textures to make the space cozier.

BEFORE

60

If you have a handful of smaller size rugs that don't fit elsewhere in the house, try overlapping them on the floor to add texture and colour, creating the look of one large rug.

LAUNDRY ROOM

We had an aha moment to turn our storage room downstairs into a laundry room. As you can see, it was dark and dingy before. Everything was haphazardly built, so this was a great opportunity to turn the room into something more functional and fabulous! We installed a couple of affordable base cabinets from IKEA with a butcher-block countertop. The washer and dryer are stacked in the corner of this tight space, allowing for a better flow. Keeping the walls mostly white and infusing bold colours on the doors and artworks make the space more lively.

DOGGY SHOWER

There was enough space in this room to add a dog shower, which is ideal for my pit bulls because they don't like being washed in the tub. Using porcelain wood-look tiles on the floor gives the texture of wood while keeping the room waterproof.

BEFORE

OUTDOOR OASIS

My backyard is a labor of love. We are spoiled with fantastic weather all year round in Los Angeles, so I spend a lot of time outside. My home is built on a slope, and the backyard is at the top, giving me a nice view of our neighborhood. When I moved in, there was a covered deck in the back with a bluish-grey railing that looked like a traditional picket fence. I decided to keep the structure of the deck railing in place and clean it up, instead of replacing it altogether. I used an airless paint sprayer and painted the fence all white to give it a lighter feeling and create a fresh canvas to work with. I chopped off the pointed picket tops of the fence posts to create a more streamlined and modern look.

Patterns and saturated hues, like greens and citrusy colours, look great in outdoor spaces. A palo verde tree in the yard served as the inspiration for this patio makeover.

The backyard has multiple areas to wander, like the covered patio, the upper lounge space, a grassy area for our pups to play or for our friends to toss some cornhole, and a succulent garden along the side with a backdrop of lush drought-tolerant plants. The backyard is an extension of our home, and we love having friends over to grill and chill.

In our succulent garden area, there were originally two mimosa trees and an overgrown dragon fruit cactus. The mimosa trees had tons of toxic seed pod droppings, and the dragon fruit was overly abundant and incredibly messy. Let's just say it wasn't the kind of fruity mimosa party I wanted in my backyard. The roots were also ruining the retaining wall, so we got rid of them and planted drought-tolerant succulents. Painting the concrete surround gives it a crisp and defined finish.

BEFORE

DAB-IT-YOURSELF
CANE LAMPSHADE

It is hard to find wall sconces or lamps with interesting shades. You can get creative and wrap a piece of cane webbing around a lampshade. It's a fun way to give your lampshade a quick and fresh update. Two popular types of cane webbing are open box weave and open weave. Here I used the open box weave because it's a tighter weave and it hides the original shade better. You can easily find cane webbing online or even on Amazon. Make sure the cane webbing matches the size of the original shade. Simply wrap the cane around your shade, and use a glue gun or staples to hold it together. You can fringe the top and bottom to add some texture as well.

DAB-IT-YOURSELF
MEDICINE CABINET

This project is more involved than a traditional DIY project, and unless you're very capable in construction, it will require someone handy or an electrician to help you. It requires creating a niche in your wall, which means you will have to open up your drywall. Once you create an opening, your electrician will mount an electrical box to the side of the niche. Then you patch it all up.

For this project I created a rectangle niche, but if your contractor is capable, you can make an arched niche to match your arched mirror. To hang the mirror, I decided to use a piano hinge and secured it to the back of the mirror, which already had a thin piece of plywood to support it, and then attached it to the left side of the niche. To add a shelf, I used a leftover piece of quartz. You can use plywood as well, which can easily be found in your local hardware store, and paint it. For the shelf pin, you will need a shelf pin drilling jig with a ¼-inch bit and pins to match the size of the hole you desire. Typically, they're around 5 millimeters in size.

MY FAMILY'S SAN GABRIEL APARTMENT

OLD

My mom, my younger sister, Elaine, and her teenage daughter (my niece, Kailey) all lived together in a tiny one-bedroom apartment in Southern California's San Gabriel Valley. It gave me flashbacks to my own crowded upbringing. To make matters worse, they amassed a lot of everything. Mountains of clothes built up on the beds and floors. Tupperware containers were stored in the oven, and every surface was covered in clutter. The apartment lacked built-in storage, but on the bright side, it had great natural light.

BRAND

My mom, Kiu, courageously immigrated to the United States from Vietnam alone in 1977. She uprooted herself and left an abusive family for a chance to start a family of her own. Kiu, Elaine, and Kailey all love clothes and shopping together. Dressing up is their favourite way of expressing themselves, and they *love* colour. I was excited to dress up their apartment to satiate their growing need for some personal space.

NEW

The plan was to help them purge, organise, and give them storage solutions. Since they love colour and weren't allowed to paint the rental, we harnessed the power of peel-and-stick wallpaper and colourful furniture and accessories to Dabify the space. Elaine and Kailey were ready for a little more autonomy, so their must-have was separate beds.

TWO GLOW-UP HOMES FOR MULTI-GENERATIONAL LIVING

MULITFUNCTIONAL LIVING ROOM

Some people collect snow globes or stamps. Well, my mom has a thing for Tupperware. There are containers of all sorts, some complete, some missing lids or bottoms, some mismatched. In addition to plastic containers, my mom also holds on to grocery bags and plastic spoons—really anything she ever comes across. It might be easy for some to think, *Just throw it all out!* But she rarely throws anything away. What I've discovered through my mom and other immigrant families and friends is that there is something comforting about holding on to things for those who have experienced trauma from being displaced. These feelings reflect a desire to save stuff for use on some far-off day in the future. My mom often holds on to things because they symbolise new memories. Since she has experienced displacement, letting go of items that have positive memories and feelings can understandably trigger anxiety.

DESIGN WITH SENSITIVITY IN MIND

I try to be sensitive to the emotional and psychological attachment my mom has to her things, but there is a line between being scrupulous and needless stockpiling. No matter how useful or beautiful something is, objects can still weigh you down and prevent you from moving on. I was watching an interview with the famous pianist and conductor Mitsuko Uchida, and she said something that really struck me: "The trouble with possessions is they end up possessing you, if you are not careful." It's a tricky balance. I mean, who am I to judge? You can see from my interiors that I'm a maximalist! But I do believe that there should be some sort of organization and order, and most importantly, beauty and intent. In my mom's case, it was chaos, and it consumed her.

To further complicate the situation, it's not easy to explain or discuss the nuance of all of this with my mom because of our language barrier. She speaks more Cantonese than English, and I speak more English than Cantonese, so we communicate with each other through acts or shared activities like cooking, eating a meal, or watching TV. As a result, starting this process with my mom was hard to navigate. We made sure we didn't talk to her in a tone that made her feel disrespected or like her feelings were being disregarded.

Interventions are never easy, but I'm happy to report that she's getting better at it each time (yes, we have been through this *multiple* times, but I'll spare you the rundown). My sister, Elaine, and I team up and tackle different corners of the apartment when my mom is away at work. We discovered after many tries that this is *our* best solution. Some people go to the Grand Canyon for family vacation; my family goes to Goodwill to make donations and let go of our physical and emotional baggage.

BEFORE

OWN YOUR SPACE
(EVEN IF YOU RENT)

My mom, Elaine, and Kailey had been living in the apartment for over ten years, but my mom still questioned why we were treating the space as if they owned it. I responded, "Mommy, it is the *only* home you have known for the past ten years." The common misconception about rentals is that because you don't have a deed to the place, you have no ownership. If you don't own the building or the unit, it doesn't mean you can't own *your* space. I believe this should be a priority the moment you move in, not a month or a year or, in my mom's case, a decade later.

The living room is a multifunctional room. A yellow sofa sleeper was the perfect solution that brightened up the space and also transformed into a bed at night for my mom. An open bookshelf acts as a divider between the living room and dining room while still maintaining a feeling of airiness in the small combined space.

We added storage in the entryway for shoes and a solution under the kitchen counter overhang to organise my mom's belongings that she insisted on keeping. For this makeover, which was completed in a week, I sourced whatever was in stock at big box stores, vintage shops, and on Craigslist. I know some high-end designers take months or years to come up with an expensive and gorgeous decor scheme, but sometimes making a place your own is about accessibility and what you can find at that very moment.

BEFORE

Lighting is a budget-friendly trick to transforming a rental space. I swapped out the tacky ceiling fan for a brass chandelier and voilà! Instant low-cost, low-effort upgrade!

BOLD BEDROOM

My sister and her daughter, Kailey, had always shared a bed. Although it is sweet to be together a lot, it also broke my heart that neither of them had ever experienced having their own private space. My niece is in middle school and desperately wanted her own room. I know exactly what she's going through because I have been there. So, one of the must-haves for this room? Separate beds!

Since my mom, sister, and niece were sharing the same closet and needed additional storage solutions, I sourced beds with drawers and added two dressers, which I positioned side by side against the wall. This not only added some serious storage, but also gave me a place to put some greenery.

When I was looking for an inexpensive bed frame that had storage underneath, two green ones caught my eye, as bold colour always does. The colourful beds led me to my next design choice—I knew we needed to use removable wallpaper to create a bold statement so that it wouldn't look like some sad rental with popcorn ceilings. When it comes to colours, I always love to play and balance warm and cool shades. Since we started with green, I picked its complementary colours, purple and magenta. I also added a floating desk in the middle so my niece can have a quiet place to study and do homework.

LET ART BE YOUR GUIDE

Many people struggle with colour, but the great thing about art is that a skilled artist has already done the work of pairing hues together for you. If you aren't sure where to start when creating a colour palette for your design, pick an artwork that speaks to you and pull colours out of it. For this room, I was inspired by an artwork that depicted a jungle scene, and from it I pulled colours to decorate the room. For instance, I chose a green headboard, burgundy and coral duvets, and a wallpaper with teal blue. These colours all work together in the room with the jungle artwork as the starting point.

BEFORE

MY FAMILY'S GLOW-UP HOME

OLD

2020 changed everyone's priorities and life in general. My mom Kiu lost her job after working tirelessly for over forty years, so she decided to retire. My sister Elaine was furloughed. And my niece Kailey started her freshman year of high school virtually. The pandemic amplified everyone's need for personal space, so we found a three-bedroom rental where they could comfortably spread out and finally have some alone time. The great thing about this ranch-style house is that it's spacious with hardwood floors, and it was newly renovated. The window treatments and the faded Creamsicle-coloured walls provided a great canvas for the GLOW UP!

BRAND

They finally had their own personal spaces and the opportunity to express their style and story. My mom loves floral patterns and is obsessed with the colour pink. She says it reminds her of her fave flower, cherry blossoms. While my mom loves colour, my sister has been really into neutrals. She went on vacay to Honolulu and stayed at a hotel completely decked out in warm whites, tans, and woods. She felt inspired and relaxed by that. And on the flip side, my niece, who is now well into her adolescence, loves everything dark and black.

NEW

Since this home is bigger than their previous abode in San Gabriel, we had to scale up their furniture. The landlord gave us permission to go wild with paint and even use traditional wallpaper to wow out the spaces. And their must-haves were bigger beds. They deserved to finally live a beautiful and luxurious life!

BRIGHT & BALANCED LIVING ROOM

Now that everyone has their own bedroom, they can all finally have a dedicated space to hang out together, so we got a comfortable sectional sofa for the living room. To build your colour confidence but keep your walls white, opt for colourful furniture and accents instead. Here, the rug serves as the colour palette for furnishings throughout. This is an example of how balanced hues from one colour palette can replace the need for a dominant colour.

BEFORE

MOM'S QUIRKY & MAXIMAL BEDROOM

WHAT WOULD DAB DO?

DISCOVER YOUR MUST-HAVES

My mom wanted a bold, cheerful bedroom that's completely different from my sister's and niece's rooms.

CREATE YOUR FLOOR PLAN

The space is a decent size with lots of windows to bring in natural light. Naturally, the bed would go against the only solid wall.

UNCOVER YOUR COLOURS

My mom has always gravitated toward colour, which is probably where I get my colour confidence from. She loves the colour yellow, and a bold pink is good luck for her. Teal and jade are found in a lot of her jewelry. I decided my two dominant colours would be yellow and pink, which are both warm and bold. To complement them, I used teal and blue accents.

SHOP TILL YOU DROP

I wanted the bed to be one of the dominant colours and found a delightful yellow bed frame with rounded edges, which makes it feel soft. To top it off, I chose a Tibetan tiger blanket to add a wild and quirky touch. The ikat throw pillows are velvet, which adds a luxurious vibe. And I found modern black nightstands to ground the space. When you have so many bright colours, black is a grounding colour that can elevate these playful colours.

MOCK IT UP

If you don't have Photoshop to mock up a mood board, you can also print out images of the pieces to help you envision the space and see how the colours, shapes, and materials all work together.

BRING ON THE BALANCE

Pink can be a tricky colour to apply in any space. I discovered a pink paint colour from Farrow & Ball called "Rangwali," which is described as an adventurous pink. And even though it's bright, it has depth with a dose of black pigment. For me, when you pick a bold colour, the only way to balance that is by picking another dominant bold colour, like the citrusy yellow in the bed. This colour combination had been on my mind ever since I saw Jil Sander's spring 2011 runway collection designed by Raf Simons.

WOW IT OUT

The focal point in any bedroom for me is the headboard wall. So, to create this stunning wow moment, we hung plates with painted peonies; found matching, floral ginger-jar lamps; and added graphic patterns.

BEFORE

HAPPY ACCIDENTS CAN MAKE FOR HAPPY ACCENTS

Keep your eyes peeled because colour and inspiration are every-where. I wasn't considering blue accents for this room until I saw painter's tape chilling on the yel-low headboard, and I loved the colour story there. I immediately went looking for vintage blue lamps. Sometimes decorating is all about happy accidents, and you have to keep your eyes open for them. They are like little gifts from styling fairies.

90

ZIEGLER RUGS

Ziegler rugs are a great choice because they don't shed like most Moroccan rugs do. They have beautiful patterns and come in many colourways. If you're looking to add colour and pattern to your space with minimal upkeep, a Ziegler rug would be a good fit because they're easy to clean. My favourite place to buy Ziegler rugs is RugSource.com. I would recommend also buying a rug pad to place underneath your rug to prevent it from slipping and to provide a bouncy, plush feel.

ELAINE'S ZEN MODERN BEDROOM

My sister, Elaine, had just turned thirty-two, and for the first time in her life she had her own bedroom, too! She truly deserves all the wonderful things. I asked her what vibe she wanted for her room, and she said Zen, modern, and natural.

She also asked for a king bed, so I gave her a woven bed frame to set the vibe for embracing all the natural materials. We kept the space minimal in colours but maximal in textures. For bedding we chose linen because it has a more relaxed feel. When working with creams, beiges, and off-whites, I like to bring in black accents to add contrast, like the bedside lamps. The Ziegler rug, while a neutral shade, has a simple graphic pattern, which adds depth to the room without overpowering.

While she wanted the room to be neutral, that doesn't mean it has to be boring. A great way to bring in some liveliness is to add plants and artwork. Yellow forsythia flower branches in a vintage Mediterranean terra-cotta vase and a *Ficus altissima* in the corner help breathe vitality into the room. Adding wallpaper to the wall behind the bed creates a focal point for the room, but when Elaine is in bed, she doesn't see it. This is a nice compromise for someone who wants a more neutral room that is still interesting and beautiful.

I used vintage Gujarat pillows from India with varying patterns on the bed, along with a throw blanket in a blue tone that reminds Elaine of a trip to Hawaii. She's beyond happy with how this turned out, and I'm thrilled she gets to call this space her own.

94

FRAME IT

I found a vintage Chinese vest while traveling in Bangkok and had it framed for this space. I had the framer float the vest in the frame and place a warm, off-white linen material behind the vest for the backing. This creates a textile-on-textile look that's much warmer than placing the vest on a normal paper mat board. I chose a black frame to tie in with the other black accents in the room and reflect the black in the vest. If you have a special textile or memento, consider framing it to create something that's personal. It could be a scarf from your great-grandmother, a shirt from your child, or a special pillowcase—whatever you choose, celebrating your memories always reflects you.

KAILEY'S SOPHISTICATED BLACK BEDROOM

While my mom and sister wanted completely light and bright rooms, my niece, Kailey, showed her individualism in requesting an all-black room. I was surprised by her bold choice and ended up loving the challenge. When painting a room black (Sherwin-Williams "Tricorn Black"), use wood and other natural tones or materials to warm up the space. The graphic wallpaper (York Wallcoverings "Sketchbook") on the ceiling helps to break up the solid black colour. It's a fun way to think outside the box and go bold. I recommend using traditional wallpaper on the ceiling because the glue creates a stronger adhesive. If you live in a place with more humidity, removable wallpaper could come down in time.

This has got to be the fanciest, most sophisticated room I've ever seen for a teenager, and I'm so happy that she got a chance to experience having her own space in these formative years.

Kailey tells me that she loves her new black bedroom. She says that when her friends come over, they think she's so fabulous!

BEFORE

HOW TO HANG PLATES

In my mom's bedroom, we had this bare pink wall above the headboard. While the room looked so much better with colour, I still wanted to jazz up the walls even more. My mom loves peonies. She'd never seen them before until we went shopping at Trader Joe's, and I grabbed a bunch for one of my photoshoots. She thinks they're more beautiful than roses because they're bigger and puffier. So, when I saw these John Derian peony plates, I knew they were the perfect way to style the wall space above her bed. Some people think plates belong in the kitchen, but I think they can go anywhere—especially if they are beautiful.

WHAT YOU'LL NEED

Disc adhesive plate hangers
(in various sizes)

Plates of your choice

Sponge

Water

Pencil

Hammer

Nails

INSTRUCTIONS

STEP 1: Adhering the plate hanger to the plate is very easy to do. The disc adhesive is a little like a stamp. Wet a sponge with a little bit of water and dab it onto the disc. Stick the disc onto the back of the plate and wait for it to dry and harden for a bit before hanging. Repeat this process for each plate you're using.

STEP 2: It's time to figure out what shape you'd like to create with your plates. I had nine plates, so I decided to create a diamond figure with the biggest plate in the centre.

STEP 3: You want to make sure you have enough space, top and bottom, for the plates. Here I allowed about 10 inches above the headboard. I pretty much eyeballed everything, leaving about 2 to 3 inches between each plate for breathing room. Using a pencil, mark where you'd like to hang each plate, and hammer in the nails accordingly. Once the nails are in place, you're ready to hang your pretty plates on the wall.

SOPHIA AND RANA'S ASTORIA CONDO

OLD

Sophia and Rana had been living in their one-bedroom condo in Astoria, New York, for over twelve years. With multiple furry babies and busy schedules, their home had gotten away from them. They were not in love with any of their oversize furniture, and there was also a lack of storage. But they love their condo and the area they live in, so they intended on living in their home for another ten years.

BRAND

Sophia and Rana work in education—she's an associate principal and he teaches science. What makes their story even sweeter is that education brought them together. They met fourteen years ago working at the same public high school in the Bronx, and they've been inseparable ever since. During their free time, Sophia loves to shop, while Rana plays basketball with his homies. Sophia has a colourful wardrobe filled with warm hues like yellows and oranges. Rana's, on the other hand, is very blue. They love traveling to tropical destinations. And they're obsessed with their furry babies.

NEW

For this project, we weren't just decorating—their condo required light renovation work to breathe some new life into the space. Sophia and Rana's to-do list included repainting the walls, refinishing the floors, updating the baseboards and doors, and adding electrical in both the living room and bedroom ceilings because they hated their existing recessed lighting. They also craved some colour in their spaces, so we aimed to balance their hues. And another one of their must-haves was a desk since they both work from home part time. I needed to come up with a multifunctional layout in the living room. It was more important than ever for them to feel like their home is a space that's inspiring and inviting—whether they're on duty or off.

A NYC CONDO WITH VACATION VIBES

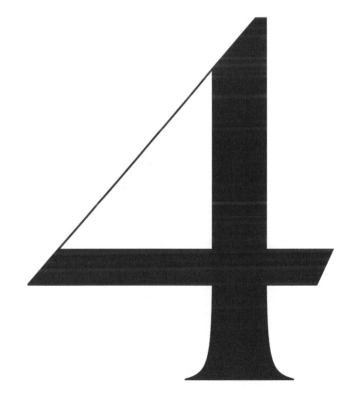

LAYERED & LAID-BACK LIVING ROOM

We had to think long and hard about how to best use this space since it's an open floor plan with the living room and kitchen together. Sophia and Rana have a huge island, which is where they eat most of their meals. They wanted to squeeze a desk in here, so we divided the living room into two spaces by placing the sofa in the middle. Rana was apprehensive about this layout (many people feel confined by walls and, more specifically, always assume that furniture needs to be placed against a wall), but after moving things around and testing it out for a few days, he said, "Why didn't we do this sooner?" Well, it's never too late! After figuring out the basic layout, it was time to have some fun with the design. Sophia loves the desert, and she wanted a warm vibe. This rust-coloured velvet sectional was one of my first choices, and everything else sort of followed from there. A comfy and stylish sofa is the centrepiece of the living room. To make it even more inviting, I added a mustard-coloured throw and pillows and layered a blue Southwest-style rug underneath.

BEFORE

106

Placing two TV consoles side by side creates a more dramatic and custom look while adding more storage. Most TV consoles are too small, adding to the garish, oversized appearance of televisions. Adding more surface area creates more space to style vases, personal photos, and other collections.

Hang your TV at eye level, which should be 8 to 10 inches above your console. This height provides the perfect orientation to build a gallery wall that will conceal your TV.

Across the room, a walnut desk with gold legs ties into the other gold elements in the room, like the desk chair, the sunburst mirror, and the modern light fixture. To make the office area feel more defined, I added a colourful Moroccan runner, and a bright graphic print above the desk to balance it all out.

To give the island a fresh look, I wrapped the base below the countertop with geometric removable wallpaper. Since all the walls are white and the furniture is mostly solid, we went with a shibori-inspired wallpaper to bring pattern into the room. It complements the hues and pattern in the rug in a pleasing way. This is a good example of pattern play: the wallpaper is white with a blue pattern and the rug is blue with a white pattern. While the patterns are not the same, pairing the two works because they're in the same colour family.

WARM & WELCOMING ENTRYWAY

Like most entryways in NYC, Sophia and Rana's is long and narrow, and it quickly filled up with clutter. A storage bench conceals shoes while providing seating.

The space was a bit dark, so we hung a large round mirror to help bounce around the existing light. It may seem counterintuitive to bring in something that doesn't help with storage, but a large white vase, bursting with flowers, conveys a sense of lightness and airiness in the dark, cramped space. The bear figurine is a personal memento they found while visiting California for the first time.

For the colour palette, we kept things mostly neutral but added hints of warm gold tones in the mirror, as well as a gold-leaf flushmount light, which made a strong statement. We layered a Peruvian-style golden-yellow runner on the floor for an easy pop of colour. To balance the warm colour scheme, I added cool tones with framed art and some photos from their travels. The front door was painted with Behr "Royal Orchard" green for an update. Since Sophia and Rana live in a condo with an HOA, we were only allowed to paint the inside of the door, which was previously a colour that didn't make them happy. This earthy green adds colour to the space while balancing the warm hues in the sofa, rugs, and other accents in the apartment. The colour green exudes that outdoor vibe and serves as a substitute for plants, which weren't really an option here due to the lack of light.

BEFORE

Rana loves basketball, so we stored a couple of balls under the console to add personality. It's a playful way to showcase a hobby. You always want your home to reflect what you love.

GOLDEN TROPICAL BEDROOM

WHAT WOULD DAB DO?

DISCOVER YOUR MUST-HAVES

Sophia and Rana wanted their bedroom to feel like they were on vacation in some tropical wonderland. A TV and dresser were musts for the space, along with a king-size bed that wasn't too high. Plus, they needed better lighting, like a chandelier and nightstand lamps.

CREATE YOUR FLOOR PLAN

The old bed frame was bulky, dark, and heavy. The headboard took up about an extra foot of usable space. When you have a small space, you want to maximise every inch. The old layout was also not ideal. I always encourage people not to have their headboard on the same wall as their bedroom door if the room allows this. I'll leave the fêng shui to the specialists, but it did make me feel really unsettled knowing they were sleeping so close to the open bedroom door, which also leads to the front door. According to fêng shui philosophy, the front door is the portal to the flow of energy, life, wealth, family, and much more. You want to harness that energy, not let it leak out through the front door. Turning the eye's focus away from the commotion of the rest of the house also promotes a calmer environment for resting.

UNCOVER YOUR COLOURS

Sophia wanted a mood booster in this space and for it to feel bespoke. Her favourite colours are rust, yellows, and pinks, and Rana seemed to like yellow as well, as long as it wasn't too bright. A mustard colour is subtle enough but still provides that energising, sunny colour. I picked out this saffron-coloured tropical wallpaper to help set the tone. To draw the eye from the walls to the bed, I chose mustard pillows and blankets. It now makes the yellow feel even more intentional.

SHOP TILL YOU DROP

We shopped for key pieces to bring this new vision to life. The tropical wallpaper from Walls Republic helped dictate the other pieces in the room. This mid-century-style chandelier above the bed is a statement piece from AllModern. The sculptural chandelier echoes the palm trees in the wallpaper, creating a bold moment.

To anchor the space below the Samsung Frame TV, I bought a faux leather bench in a green shade that works nicely with the wallpaper. If you plan on mounting a TV on the wall, make sure you shop for a pretty basket to hide the wires and the router.

Sophia and Rana needed storage in this room, so we found a mid-century-style dresser to place on the opposite wall. Finding nightstands with drawers also added more storage. To add more personal details and carry out the vacation vibes, we framed photos Sophia and Rana snapped during their travels.

BEFORE

MOCK IT UP

For this mock-up, I asked Sophia and Rana to be part of the process, and I had them print out pictures of some of the pieces we were considering for this space so they could visualise the room. This allowed them to have some say and ownership in their bedroom. For instance, we were considering green or blue lamps for the nightstands, and once they saw how the blue lamps interacted with other elements in the room, they were sold on them.

BRING ON THE BALANCE

The bedroom originally had matching furniture sets, which I am never a fan of because I like to see a variety of unique pieces that make a statement or proclaim your personality in a room. A predetermined set feels too dorm-like, and that's not the vibe they were going for. With a bold wallpaper, we brought in a neutral rug and a solid-coloured, tall headboard. With the warm colours of the wallpaper, we needed some cool tones and picked out these blue ceramic lamps for the nightstands. Play with lighter and darker shades of wood within a space—they don't all have to match.

WOW IT OUT

Installing wallpaper on all the walls immerses you into this tropical paradise right when you walk through the door. The bed and headboard area serves as the focal point and draws attention immediately. When looking to create a wow moment in a bedroom, placing the bed on the wall opposite the door, along with a fantastic headboard, wallpaper, and display of artwork, will always command focus and invite you in.

RYAN'S NEW ORLEANS HOME

OLD

It was only four months into our relationship when my husband, Ryan (also lovingly referred to as my favourite client), decided to become a first-time homeowner and bought a 1950s ranch-style home in New Orleans. Though it was a great house, it didn't come without some flaws. All the interior walls were painted a morose light grey colour, which prompted me to make the joke that I brought LA smog with me into his New Orleans house. The dining room was very dark because it was in the middle of the home and had no windows. The bathroom had dated mosaic tiles, and the backyard had a rundown shed with zero plants. But there was one room with three large picture windows that brought in natural light so we immediately called it the sunroom. Let the inspiration flow and the glow up begin!

BRAND

After an epic five-day first date in Montauk and another lovely ten-day second date in New Orleans, I decided on our third date that I'd move to New Orleans to live with my boo. When you know, you know! What I didn't know was that I was moving in with a difficult CLIENT. I'm teasing. Since our relationship was very new, it was fun getting to know Ryan and helping him decorate his new home. I discovered that we share an affinity for textiles and traveling. He traveled to Istanbul and bought some beautiful Turkish rugs and pillows a couple years back. His favourite colours are navy blue, Kelly green, and coral. He loves antiquing as well. He loves to hike, and the beach is his favourite place to relax.

NEW

Ryan's home is 2,100 square feet, which I considered to be a fairly big space that would need a lot of furniture. The plan was to source from local vintage stores for deals because we were on a shoestring budget. At the top of the to-do list was painting over all the grey walls, creating a space plan that would make the parlor room warm and inviting, and making the dining room stand out. The outdoor space needed a ton of plants, and the shed needed to be removed to make a patio for outdoor entertaining.

A BUDGET-FRIENDLY MAKEOVER FOR A FIRST-TIME HOMEOWNER

GLOBAL-INSPIRED LIVING ROOM

If you have high ceilings, adding stained glass above a doorway will bring an unexpected dose of colour.

This expansive parlor room was a challenge. My design anchor was a beautiful vintage Van Dyver-Witt striped sofa that echoes the same colours that are in the stained glass above the doorway. With such a big space like this that also boasts a fireplace, tons of windows, an entryway, and an archway, the only way for the layout to work was to place the sofa in the middle of the room. You can see that I had to fill each corner to make this large space feel cozier.

In a sea of earthy tones, painting the front door a Kelly green (Ryan's favourite colour) adds a bold impact to the space. I couldn't find a big enough rug within the budget, so I got two 9 by 12-foot jute rugs to create an illusion of a large rug and then layered an 8 by 10-foot rug over them to add more colour and pattern.

After visiting South Africa, I brought home eight Binga baskets—I was inspired by the Saxon Hotel in Johannesburg where there was an entire wall filled with them.

BEFORE

RADIANT YELLOW DINING ROOM

WHAT WOULD DAB DO?

DISCOVER YOUR MUST-HAVES

This room was my first time participating in the One Room Challenge, which is a design makeover competition that invites designers to give a single room a transformation in six weeks' time. I love to layer bold on top of bold on top of bold, so I was excited to work within that time frame to create a maximal space.

The dining room was off to the side of the parlor, and it had zero windows. Ryan never used this room before because it wasn't exciting or inspiring to be in there. And even though he painted it white, it still felt dark. He wanted a vibrant room where he could host people and have fun parties. He also wanted a bigger dining table and an elegant chandelier.

CREATE YOUR FLOOR PLAN

The floor plan for this room was straightforward. The dining room had two entryways, so it made sense to place the buffet against the shorter wall, because the room was long and narrow. And the dining table was centreed in the room and anchored by a 9 by 12-foot rug.

UNCOVER YOUR COLOURS

Ryan wanted a room that screamed, "Come in here and have a mimosa!" He loves brunch, especially poached eggs. So, we had a silly idea of making a dining room inspired by yolk.

BEFORE

SHOP TILL YOU DROP

If you find that painting an entire room is too bold, then adding artworks can help tone that down. I searched for New Orleans abstract artists through Where Y'Art Works, a local art gallery, and discovered the artist, Leroy Miranda Jr. I had custom wall-mount candleholders made by Sazerac Stitches. Captain chairs were also on the shopping list, and I wanted them to be a different shape than the green upholstered chairs. We went with black chairs with hard edges and vertical spindles, which balance out the soft elements in the room and tie in with the rug, chandelier, artworks, and sconces.

MOCK IT UP

I created a quick copy-and-paste mock-up in Photoshop.

BRING ON THE BALANCE

A cheerful yellow paint colour brightens the once-dark space, which is accented with colourful abstract artworks, blue accessories, and green to balance the warm and cool tones in the design. Balance is about juxtaposition of styles. Because the new molding makes the space feel more traditional, we chose a sculptural chandelier to give it a contemporary update.

WOW IT OUT

The wow moment here is when you see the room framed from the living room, so I wanted this to be major. This Caracas chandelier from Jonathan Adler elevated the space with its brass finish. It has an air of formality, yet it remains fun and unexpected. The yellow paint colour transformed the dining room into a welcoming and cheerful room. We added a chair rail and molding (see page 152) to bring sophistication to the space, while the mix of artworks adds personality.

COSY & COLOURFUL SUNROOM

When Ryan first moved in, he considered making the sunroom the dining room. But because it has beautiful natural light, we turned this into a TV room/den. Dark navy walls lend a bold contrast to the other areas of the brightly coloured home and make this space feel more intimate. People often feel scared painting walls dark because they're afraid it will make a space feel smaller and more enclosed, when in reality it can make a space feel cozier. And let's be real, no amount of paint will ever change the actual square footage of a space.

FIND YOUR ACCENT COLOURS FROM THE GROUND UP

When choosing colours for throw pillows, think about picking out accent shades from the patterns in your rug and repeat them in your pillows to add cohesion to your space. Just like when you see an artwork with colour combinations that inspire your space's colour palette, you can echo pleasing colour pairings you see in one place somewhere else in the same room. If your rug has warm accent colours like yellow and red, think about using those colours in the throw pillows on your sofa.

BEFORE

LIGHT & ENERGETIC CORNER DESK

Next to the sunroom is my office nook. It was an unused, awkward corner, so I made a DIY desk wall unit to utilise the once-dead space more efficiently. (See Dab-It-Yourself: Desk Wall Unit, page 150.) The shelves are filled with plants, art supplies, and cameras to foster creative energy. Vintage hand-carved Senufo stools are perfect for stacking books. I placed a vibrant red Moroccan rug underneath because red is a symbol of vitality and prosperity in Chinese culture.

PATTERNED PRIMARY BEDROOM

Ryan's bedroom was awash in a sea of sad grey scale. He didn't even have nightstands. That's not how a bedroom should ever be. We brought the tropical relaxation vibes to the bedroom by installing a lush wallpaper behind the bed to make an accent wall.

GRAPHIC EN SUITE BATHROOM

For the en suite bathroom, I was inspired by the patterns and movements in the two artworks by SheShe. We removed the tub and created a standing shower to open up the space. The cement cube tiles on the wall are the first thing you see in the bathroom and set a bold scene. Taking a cue from the artwork on top, we chose to paint the vanity a jade colour.

I love including wood elements in a bathroom to warm up a typically cold, tiled, marbled space. These octagonal wood mirrors also add an earthiness and unique sculptural shape.

BEFORE

TEXTILE-FILLED GUEST BEDROOMS

OPPOSITE: For the first guest bedroom, a 9 by 12-foot rug was used to cover beige carpet. This instantly created a bold impact. When it comes to styling a bed, I like to match the artwork, throw pillows, and bed coverlet in the same colour to create a strong colour story. The artwork above the bed was intended to be vertical, but I decided to flip it horizontally. There are no rules—it's your space. If you need to turn art on its side to fit better in your space, then do you, boo.

LEFT: The small guest room had an awkward layout with closets on one side, windows on two of the walls, and a door on the fourth wall, so the only option was to put a bed in front of the window. I sprinkled lots of my Moroccan finds into this space and reimagined the headboard by using two unused couch cushions.

CORAL-SPLASHED MUDROOM

Here's how to make a huge impact on your mudroom or back entrance without breaking the bank: add a splash of colour to your door. And don't play it safe when there are so many fun colours out there to choose from! For the mudroom, I painted the door Sherwin-Williams "Dishy Coral" since the front door is Kelly green (yin and yang). Pick a graphic rug that's got a hint of that paint colour to tie the room together. A shelving unit doubles as a shoe rack and a place to drop sunglasses and mail on the way in the door. A green metal chair for seating is both a functional place to put on shoes and draws the green tones from the artwork, plants, and decor for a cohesive final touch.

BEFORE

Add a tall vase with a sculptural plant like this
Chinese fan palm to draw the eye up and add
visual interest.

CHEERFUL CURB APPEAL

To add much-needed curb appeal, we planted ferns, philodendrons, and ginger plants to fill up the front. The railing and poles were painted white and the front door a bright and happy yellow (Sherwin-Williams "Cadence"). The front door is a great way to begin using colour in small but impactful doses. What could be a more cheerful way to enter your home than by a sunshine portal?

PAINTING THE FRONT DOOR TWO COLOURS

While my front door is Sherwin-Williams "Cadence" yellow from the outside, I painted it Sherwin-Williams "Kilkenny" green on the inside. This is a reminder that your door colour doesn't have to be the same on both sides. So have fun with it.

BEFORE

MOROCCAN-INSPIRED BACKYARD

There was a preexisting shed and patio in the back, but it was in total disrepair, having withstood the beating of time, weather, and termites. Our goal was to have an outdoor space for lounging and entertaining—essentially an extension of our living space that's warm and cosy. I have to say, this was a true collaboration with my husband, as he was the one who came up with the design.

We gutted the shed, kept the foundation, and constructed a covered patio that is 11 feet high. The roof is slightly slanted, so it drains rainwater to the back. The corner wall was Ryan's brilliant move to create more privacy, since it led into our side alley.

Here's an easy DIY (see page 148) that made a huge impact. To save money, I painted the concrete floors white and then stencilled a Moroccan pattern onto them. I decided to use two colours of blue to create variation. I was inspired by my trip to Chefchaouen, which is Morocco's Blue City. The blue is supposed to ward off mosquitos, and there are a lot of them in New Orleans. I am a mosquito magnet so I need all the help I can get.

For a bold and dramatic look, we stained the fence black. Black stain has a softer look than black paint because it shows the wood grain. And using black outdoors is a great way to create a beautiful backdrop for your vibrant green plants, as it amplifies and dramatises the greenery.

BEFORE

DAB-IT-YOURSELF
TWO WAYS TO STYLE A KING BED

MINIMAL

2 KING PILLOWS + 1 LUMBAR PILLOW + 1 DUVET + 1 COVERLET

Lay duvet and tuck it all the way to the headboard. Place two king pillows flat side down. Add interest by tossing a lumbar pillow in front of them. Layer a patterned coverlet at the end of the bed, covering one-third or half of it. I like to match the colours of the coverlet with the lumbar for cohesion. And that's it! Now you've got an effortlessly chic bed.

MAXIMAL

2 KING PILLOWS + 2 STANDARD PILLOWS + 2 ACCENT PILLOWS + 1 LUMBAR PILLOW + 1 DUVET + 1 COVERLET + 1 THROW

First, lay duvet down all the way to the headboard, then fold duvet back about 20 inches to create room for pillows. Prop up two king pillows against the headboard. Put two standard pillows in front of them. Here I have one standard pillow in white and the other in navy sham. Weave in two throw pillows, overlapping the king and standard pillows. Then toss a lumbar pillow in front. Layer a coverlet on half of the bed. Loosely drape a throw across the coverlet for an accent. For colours, I matched the coverlet to the colours of the pillows and the throw to the lumbar pillow to create cohesion.

DAB-IT-YOURSELF
PAINTED FLOOR TILES

If you don't have the dough to wow out your patio floors with tiles, you'll be surprised by how much impact stenciling can make. Our patio is 300 square feet. If we actually tiled this baby using Granada Tile, it would've cost about $5,000 just for the tiles alone. This project took me two full days, and it was a real test of my patience. Remember that I'm an Aries and patience is not one of my strengths. Whew! But you know what? It reminded me of inking and pulling prints in the printmaking studios, which I loved. Stenciling is pretty straightforward, and the outcome is rewarding.

WHAT YOU'LL NEED

Tile stencil

Exterior paint (Sherwin-Williams "Snowbound," Sherwin-Williams "Adriatic Sea," and Sherwin-Williams "In the Navy")

Paint roller (I used a 4-inch roller)

Scrap cardboard (for wiping the stencil clean)

Rags (for wiping excess paint)

Clear matte natural paver sealer

INSTRUCTIONS

STEP 1: Make sure concrete is clean before painting it white. Let it dry for twenty-four hours before stenciling.

STEP 2: Start at a corner. Lay your stencil on top of the concrete and apply a light but even coat of exterior paint using the paint roller. Let dry. In between painting each tile, transfer the stencil to a piece of cardboard and wipe it clean with a rag so there is no excess paint drip.

STEP 3: Apply a second coat of paint to each tile. Make sure to continue cleaning the stencil between painting each tile using the cardboard and a rag.

STEP 4: When all the painting is finished and your tiles are dry, apply four coats of clear matte natural paver sealer. It has a milky look when you first pour it onto the concrete, but it dries completely clear without bubbling. I was able to squeeze four coats (allowing 1 hour for drying in between each) from 2 gallons.

I love the subtle colour variations from tile to tile. It looks very hand painted (and it was!). You'll notice that my edges and lines aren't super straight or crisp. The concrete floor was old, porous, and bumpy, so it was hard to achieve that. Spacing was off here and there, but I wasn't trying to be a perfectionist about it. Embrace those happy flaws! It's very—how do you say—wabi-sabi? I love it, and it totally transforms the space. It has a modern Mediterranean feel to it now.

DAB-IT-YOURSELF
DESK WALL UNIT

An unused and weird wall space can be the perfect spot for a custom desk. Inspired by Danish mid-century-modern teak wall units, this is giving Poul Cadovius vibes at a fraction of the cost.

This affordable DIY version can look expensive (a little gold spray paint goes a long way!) but costs you around $200 to achieve. By using modular shelving brackets, you can customise your desk wall unit to be as large or small as you need for your own space.

Note: The measurements provided below are for the desk wall unit you see in this space, but feel free to create your own custom configuration.

WHAT YOU'LL NEED

1 can Rust-Oleum primer spray paint

2 cans Rust-Oleum gold metallic spray paint

4 (70-inch) Rubbermaid twin track uprights

17 (11.5-inch) Rubbermaid twin track shelf brackets

3 (18.5-inch) Rubbermaid twin track shelf brackets

Leveler

Pencil

Tape measure

¼-inch drill bit, for the anchors

Power drill

Hammer

5 Rubbermaid twin track hardware packs (I used typical drywall anchors and gold screws instead of the ones that came in the pack)

4 (12 by 24-inch) Rubbermaid shelves

3 (12 by 48-inch) Rubbermaid shelves

1 (¾ by 20 by 48-inch) sheet of plywood (this is your desk surface)

INSTRUCTIONS

STEP 1: Spray-paint the tracks and brackets outdoors. I applied a layer of primer first, then two layers of gold. They will dry pretty quickly but be gentle with them, as they can scratch.

STEP 2: I started with the left track. Depending on your ceiling height (mine is 9 feet), place the track 21 inches off the floor, vertically. Use a leveler to make sure the track is straight. Then, use a pencil to mark each hole. Once you have the holes marked from the first track, use a tape measure to measure 22 inches to the right from those marks. Place the next track 21 inches off the floor, vertically, using a leveler to make sure it's straight. Mark the holes with a pencil. Repeat this two more times.

STEP 3: Use a ¼-inch drill bit to drill into all the marked spots on the wall. Don't let the size of the bit intimidate you. You can easily patch it up later on. Gently hammer the anchors into the wall. Then line up each track over the anchors and screw them in using a power drill.

STEP 4: Pop the shelf brackets into the tracks to your desired shelving configuration. Then place your wooden shelves and your sheet of plywood (this is your desk surface) on them. For standard desk height, measure 29 inches from the floor. There are countless ways to configure the shelves, so it's really up to you if you want to include a desk or just shelves.

STEP 5: Be sure to use gold screws to secure the brackets to the shelves.

And that's it! It took me a couple hours to do this alone, but if you have help, it'll be quicker.

DAB-IT-YOURSELF
PANEL MOLDING

Panel molding is a trim that goes over a flat wall to add interest. It adds dimension and depth to rather boring spaces with no existing architectural details.

WHAT YOU'LL NEED

Picture frame molding

Measuring tape

Pencil

Miter saw

Wall paint(s)

Leveler

Nail gun

Air compressor

Nails

Primer

Caulk (Sherwin-Williams sells a quick-dry version)

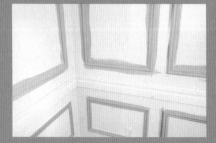

INSTRUCTIONS

STEP 1: Measuring the panel took me a while to figure out. Many homeowners have their chair rails land 36 inches up the wall from the floor, but that felt way too high for our 9-foot ceiling. After some research, I found that 28 to 32 inches was the right height. And when in doubt, it's better to err on the lower side. Since we were putting panel molding above and below the chair rail, I decided to go with 32 inches from the floor. For each wall, I went with an odd number of panels in alternating widths to give it more visual interest. The spacing between each panel is 4 inches. This means that on our longest wall (184 inches), there are five panels up above the chair rail and five panels mirroring the same width below it. The panel width size varies from wall to wall because each wall has different dimensions, but I kept all the smaller panels at 22 inches wide and worked the larger ones around them just to give them some consistency. I made all of my panel adjustments by using a miter saw to cut each piece. And then I painted the top yellow and the bottom white to create more contrast in this room.

STEP 2: When you nail in your chair rail, it's important to find the studs, which are typically 16 inches apart. Using your leveler and tape measure, measure out your trim pieces and mark their placement on your wall with a pencil. Connect the nail gun to the air compressor and use your nail gun and nail each trim piece to the wall, following your pencil markings.

STEP 3: Once all the trims are up, it's priming and caulking time. The outlets were a pain in the butt because they were in the way, so I decided to have the molding go around them. It would've cost a few hundred dollars more, as well as taken more time just to raise them, so I wasn't about to do that. Wall trims make a huge difference in a space. If you want to make your room feel more custom, this is an easy trick to jazz it up.

ANNA AND RYAN'S MONTEREY PARK HOME

OLD

Anna and her husband, Ryan, bought their two-bedroom turnkey home in Monterey Park, California, in 2012. When they moved in, they never figured out a space plan or even thought about what kind of vibe or colours they wanted to bring into their space. And after a decade, they'd accumulated a lot of things, which took over their living spaces. It was complete chaos with empty shoe boxes piled all the way to the ceiling, shopping bags crunched up in every corner, and mountains of random stuff. This was definitely not the wow moment we wanted to create. The living spaces and even the bathroom lacked good flow. It was clear that storage was an issue. But underneath all the layers of clutter was actually a charming space with original hardwood floors and huge windows that let in tons of sunlight.

BRAND

Anna and Ryan had a beautiful wedding in Hawaii. And they go back every year because Ryan has family there. It's their favourite place to escape, to relax, and to eat delicious musubi, fresh seafood, and sweet flavours of shave ice. Hawaii is where their heart is, and I was determined to infuse that magical place into their home.

NEW

Their homework was to go through their belongings and purge all the boxes, empty bags, and junk that added no value or joy to their lives. Anna and Ryan wanted to renovate their bathroom to make it more functional with a double sink and a closet for storage. This was a case where they needed to let go of old junk in order to bring in new energy and balance to their lives.

GROWING A FAMILY & DECLUTTERING IN A CALIFORNIA HOME

6

RELAXED COASTAL LIVING ROOM

Anna and Ryan's living room was filled with clutter. They had accumulated and accumulated, never getting rid of anything because they truly believed that their stuff would one day come in handy. It reminded me of my mom's place and her mentality. This is clearly a generational problem that affects the children of immigrants, too. So, how do we break this cycle? I don't have the answers. Therapy might be helpful. But I can give you some therapeutic advice. It starts by recognising how clutter makes us feel anxious and overwhelmed. It takes practice and maintenance, just like working out or having your car tuned up.

I asked Anna and Ryan if they wanted a beautiful home for their children to grow up in, where they can have their own space and have friends over. And if they could make all the things they don't really love disappear so they can start anew, would they do it? Their answers were a resounding yes.

Since they visit Hawaii every year for vacation, we infused an eclectic, beachy, laid-back vibe. The colour story for their living room was ocean blue and sandy browns with a hint of sunshine yellow.

BEFORE

For the layout, since there are windows on one wall and two archways opposite each other, the only way to place the pair of sofas was in the middle of the room facing one another. This creates a more intimate and cosy environment.

SUNSET DINING ROOM

Here's the thing: Anna and Ryan don't have a specific style, nor do they collect art or objects. For the colour story, we took inspiration from a photo of Anna and Ryan's favourite shave ice shop in Hawaii. I loved the warm coral mixed with the cool shades of blue. We matched the colours from the inspo photo and painted the walls Behr "Terra Cotta Clay" and hung artworks with hints of blue in them. We swapped the ceiling fan/light fixture for a woven, blue-striped pendant to add a warm, graphic, and textural touch. To tackle the flooring, which Ryan admittedly hated, we found an area rug to disguise the tiles. Using the rug to carry the colour through still gives that dramatic coral splash when you enter the room.

FOOD FOR THOUGHT

When you're seeking colour inspiration, look to your favourite meals, restaurants, and food memories. Whether you're drawn to the colour of mint or eggplant, a special soup your mom makes, or a shave ice you had on vacation in Hawaii, the things we eat can spark creative colour stories.

BEFORE

FRESH & FUNCTIONAL BATHROOM

The bathroom needed to be reconfigured to a more functional layout. We updated the tub and hooked them up with the whole waterworks, including a handheld showerhead. We converted their old walk-in shower into a closet because they desperately need more storage space. The vanity and toilet were moved to the wider wall of the bathroom, to create better flow and usability. We also installed two arched mirrors to replace the tiny medicine cabinet that was installed way too high. Anna is only 4 feet 11 inches, so she needed a proper mirror hung at the right height.

This room itself wasn't that interesting to begin with so I added prism mosaic tiles from Floor & Decor to make the space more visually exciting. You can never go wrong with a tumbling tile pattern. We didn't want the room to be too white, but we didn't want it to feel too dark either, so an accent wall was a great way to add interest without being overwhelming.

We chose simple, modern pieces from Mitzi for the lighting. The shower surround has classic subway tiles with white grout and a niche, and we also added recessed lighting in there. For most of the fixtures, we stuck with gold tones. I love the warmth gold adds to a bathroom.

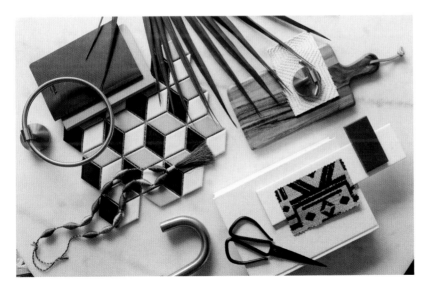

BEFORE

NUDE BEACHY BEDROOM

For the bedroom, we created a sensual and calming space. First, I chose abstract diptychs that have a calming effect and were inspired by the Santa Cruz coastline. Then I picked a paint colour that complements the artworks. I chose Farrow & Ball "Setting Plaster" which is a nude, dusty pink and painted the walls, ceiling, and trims for a tonal look. I hung the large artworks off-centre to create a more dynamic visual style. To add height and balance on the other side of the room, I went to the yard and foraged a jacaranda branch and placed it in a tall ceramic vase. For bedding, muted, Neapolitan ice cream tones in bone, rose, and chocolate stripes echo the tones from the artworks. It's a delicious colour combo that just works!

WHIMSICAL NURSERY

WHAT WOULD DAB DO?

DISCOVER YOUR MUST-HAVES

Just one year after I transformed their bedroom, Anna and Ryan were expecting their first child. I'm not gonna take full credit (because we can thank modern science for that), but I do think that by finally letting go of things that served no purpose other than crowding their mental and physical space, Anna and Ryan created an opening for new life. For their nursery, they wanted the typical nursery essentials and a crib that converts into a bed when their child grows older. But, most importantly, they wanted their daughter, Riley, to have a room where she can play and grow without any clutter.

CREATE YOUR FLOOR PLAN

We decided to position the crib along the largest wall in the room. All other furniture was placed along the adjacent walls to allow plenty of room for Riley to crawl and play as she gets older.

UNCOVER YOUR COLOURS

When Anna was carrying her baby, she had these sudden cravings for peaches and nectarines, so that led to the inspiration for the room. Sometimes the colour story can be as simple as something you crave eating. So, if you feel stuck on a colour palette, think of some of your favourite things to eat.

SHOP TILL YOU DROP

We searched high and low for a wallpaper that would grow with Riley and not feel too childish over time. Wallpaper and installation can be expensive, so carefully choose a pattern that will feel timeless and get you the most bang for your buck. We wanted the wallpaper in this room to feel gender neutral, so we chose a pattern with Japanese cranes against blue skies and peachy, cloud-like trees. To cover up an old carpet, you can use Moroccan rugs in playful and colourful designs. They are perfect for children's rooms because they feel whimsical yet elevated.

MOCK IT UP

When I was coming up with the design for this room, I created a Pinterest board and shared it with Anna and Ryan. Since I mostly designed this room remotely, Pinterest was an easy and effective way to share my vision for the room and let Anna and Ryan weigh in with their own ideas. This is a great way for you to plan and visualise your own space before you make any big design decisions.

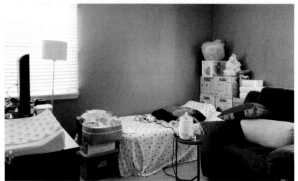

BEFORE

BRING ON THE BALANCE

Since the wallpaper has such a dominant pattern, I wanted to let it do most of the talking in the room while informing the other decor. We chose a lot of accent pieces in solid colours, like the cream rocker, the blush pouf, and the mauve canopy. Bringing in natural textures with neutral tones through baskets and wood rounds out the space without feeling too busy.

WOW IT OUT

The pièce de résistance in this space is the crib and wallpaper. I wanted to accentuate the crib even more by adding a canopy. However, I did do some research after I styled this space and found that it can be a safety hazard to hang a canopy over a crib. I don't have kids, so I didn't know! But after decorating my first nursery, I definitely had mild baby fever!

170

DAB-IT-YOURSELF
FIBER ART

Making your own piece of art and hanging it in your home is one of the best ways to make your home feel personal. And it's easy and affordable! I started creating these simple fiber drawings on paper in 2010 because I had a lot of printmaking papers left over from college and didn't want them to go to waste. Instead of using watercolours, I wanted to try something different. I remember fiber art was just starting to get popular again, and I was inspired by a fiber piece I found from a thrift store.

WHAT YOU'LL NEED

Thick art paper, such as watercolour or printmaking paper

Pencil

Scrap paper

2-millimeter-thick string or yarn (in various colours)

2-inch tapestry needle

Scissors

INSTRUCTIONS

STEP 1: Making these fiber drawings is very simple. You will need thick art paper like watercolour paper or printmaking paper. The Arches BFK Rives line has some good options. For this project I used Somerset Velvet. You can usually find these at an art store or online.

STEP 2: Use a pencil to sketch random shapes on a separate piece of paper first to get an idea of your design. Once you have your design figured out, lightly draw your loose shapes and lines on the art paper to help guide you.

STEP 3: Thread your string through the needle, and then simply poke through the paper with the needle and string to make basic embroidery stitches. I mostly do straight lines in fun geometric shapes. I don't usually cut the string too long, otherwise it can get all tangled. It's easier to work with a shorter string, about 24 inches.

STEP 4: Once that's finished, I tie a knot and trim the end. Then I rethread another one and go from there. You can also play around with letting some strings hang loosely.

DABITO'S LA GUEST HOUSE

OLD

What really sold me on my LA house was the ADU (accessory dwelling unit). It's about 300 square feet, but it was an awkward space that was used as a laundry room and storage room. There was mismatched flooring with concrete on one side and linoleum on the other. It had no windows. But I saw its potential as a rental for extra income or even as my art studio.

BRAND

One of my dreams is to one day design a boutique hotel. I've always loved the idea of hosting and creating a fun experience for people. I imagined that this would be like a great getaway for my friends and family or even for myself, to be honest. I would name it the Sterling Guesthouse after one of our pups. I was inspired by the San Francisco Proper Hotel designed by Kelly Wearstler. She used a lot of vintage artworks and geometric shapes, and paired blush velvet sofas with greens and yellows, which is very me in style. So, I decided to lean into that with this project.

NEW

My plan was to take down the dividing wall and turn this into one big studio space. We wanted to add a kitchenette, a small bathroom, a bed, and a corner desk to transform this into a small but mighty multifunctional space. Because there was a lot going into this, we needed to create a floor plan to find the best flow and then mock it up to make sure that everything would fit and balance beautifully.

300 SQUARE FEET OF MULTI-FUNCTIONAL PERSONALITY

TWO-TONED KITCHENETTE

WHAT WOULD DAB DO?

DISCOVER YOUR MUST-HAVES

For this kitchenette, I wanted open shelving up top and cabinets on the bottom with an overhang counter for dining.

CREATE YOUR FLOOR PLAN

Since the room has an open floor plan, this was a tricky space to lay out, but with some imagination we made it multifunctional. Colour defines each area, and the rugs in each space have different patterns, establishing a different personality from the living area to the kitchen and so on. If you're looking to designate different spaces within an open concept, a good way to mix and match rugs is to pull the same colour or tones through each rug in the space. This makes them feel separate yet unified.

UNCOVER YOUR COLOURS

I was set on green cabinets from day one and found this beautiful olive-green colour called "Fig Tree" by Behr, which was kismet because there is a big fig tree outside as you approach the guesthouse. And the yellow tiles are my original designs in a collaboration with SABA Tile Company. To define this space, I painted the upper wall a pistachio green. Fig and pistachios are delicious together, right? Another room inspired by foods!

SHOP TILL YOU DROP

I looked for prefabricated cabinets that were in stock at hardware stores, which made installation quick. The quartz countertop slab I sourced for a song. Then I found a long oak shelf that spanned the entire countertop to add storage. Two large sconces lend a bold statement to this small space.

MOCK IT UP

I mocked this up in Photoshop. Initially I had selected different tiles and sconces for the kitchenette area, so it's fun to look back and see how my design changed from the mock-up to the final look.

BRING ON THE BALANCE

The tone-on-tone paint colour treatment is visually broken up by the graphic tiles, giving the eye an interesting but calming place to rest. Wood tones add an earthy, soft element to the space and run the whole length of the cabinets through a decorative wooden shelf. Brass and black accents complement one another, and the brass serves as a warm tone that balances out the cool green cabinets.

WOW IT OUT

I wanted the entire kitchenette to feel like a wow moment. From the graphic tiles to the sconces, the hexagonal hardware to the tone-on-tone green effect, and everything in between, this kitchenette is small but mighty.

BEFORE

PAINTING YOUR CABINETS: A CAUTIONARY TALE

The idea of painted cabinets is exciting! If prefabricated painted cabinets are not in the cards for you, painting your existing cabinets might seem appealing. But you need to know the facts before you hit your cabinets with a bucket of paint. Make sure to sand and prime the cabinets before painting. For best results, use a durable paint, like enamel cabinet paint in a semigloss or high-gloss finish. For this project, I used a foam roller to paint the outer surface boxes and a paint spray gun for the doors and drawers for a smooth finish all around. This was my first time painting cabinets, and I honestly would leave it to professionals next time for a cleaner, smoother finish. Paint takes about a month to cure, so don't go filling up the cabinets right away—you'll know if that's impractical for your household. I've already made a few dings on mine. Even after correctly following all the steps for priming, painting, drying, and curing, this is a high-traffic part of the home, so dings and scratches will be inevitable if you choose to paint the cabinets—whether it's you or a professional who does the job.

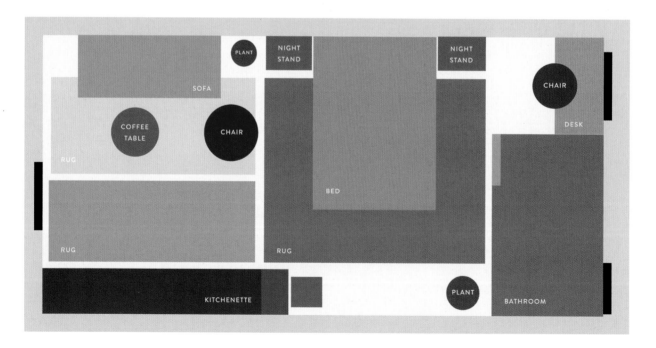

TRANSITIONAL LIVING SPACE & BEDROOM

On the other side of the kitchenette, the living space is equally rich in colour. We went bold with a velvet yellow-ochre sofa but toned it down with neutral and monochromatic pillows. Depending on the time of the day and the lighting, the colour and texture of velvet change subtly. This sofa ranges in tone from ochre to saffron to amber to olive green.

Right next to the living area is the bedroom. We picked out a low-profile queen-size bed and draped the headboard with indigo fabric designed by Justina Blakeney. Initially, I wanted to staple it tautly to the back of the headboard, but I ended up loving the loose and laid-back drapery effect on the sides. Sometimes you can add pattern to your headboard without reupholstering.

RISE & SHINE BATHROOM

If you have a lot of white walls in your home, a great way to experiment with bold colour is by using it in a small space, like a bathroom. This yellow paint colour by Behr called "Lamplit" provides a warm and happy vibe. Black-and-white Moroccan tiles add more character and interest to the bathroom without competing with the paint colour. I had the shower tiles installed vertically to give a clean and fresh take on classic subway tiles.

WHEN IN DOUBT, MATCH YOUR GROUT

If the slightest imperfections bug you, choose a grout colour that matches your tiles. It will hide any tiles that appear to look slightly off, which can happen even when a pro does your installation. One day I came home to a tile installation that looked off to me, but the work was already done. To troubleshoot, I had my installer use white grout on the white tiles, instead of a black grout, to mask the imperfections with a visual illusion.

BIEN'S JERSEY CITY APARTMENT

OLD

Bien lives in Jersey City in a one-bedroom apartment. It previously had dated track lighting and dingy blue carpet. Most of his furniture were hand-me-downs from his relatives who happened to live in the building next door. He never prioritised his space, even though it was a decent size.

BRAND

Bien enjoys visiting Baguio, a mountain town that has learned to adapt with the modern times while respecting the importance of traditions, in the Philippines. It's a booming city but abundant in lush greenery. To find the perfect complement to his penchant for the colour green, we chose his mom's favourite colour, purple. His favourite vacation spot is either a beach town somewhere in Southeast Asia, somewhere tropical yet cooled by the ocean air and surrounded by the greens of a jungle, or the desert of Joshua Tree for camping.

NEW

The plan was to remove all the track lighting, give the walls a fresh coat of paint, and update the window treatments. I wanted to sell his old furniture and accessories on Facebook Marketplace and OfferUp so that Bien could have a fresh start with new pieces that speak to his style. His must-have was a corner where he could work and enjoy a home-cooked dinner. He also wanted to host friends because he was getting tired of always making the trek to NYC to meet friends for dinner. Lastly, I wanted to sprinkle in all the souvenirs Bien's collected from his travels to reflect his free-spirited personality.

TWO RADICAL RENTAL TRANSFORMA-TIONS

NEUTRAL MAXIMAL LIVING ROOM

WHAT WOULD DAB DO?

DISCOVER YOUR MUST-HAVES

Bien was ready to let go of all his hand-me-down furniture to create a multifunctional living room and a dining-room nook that could also double as a work space. The room needed a fresh coat of paint, but I didn't use just some ordinary paint. I chose Portola Paints & Glazes limewash to help give more character and depth. Limewash is a specialty finish that requires a different process of painting. You can see how much texture and variation it added to the walls. It's a great way to make your space that much more interesting.

CREATE YOUR FLOOR PLAN

We divided the room in two. The goal was to create a stylish, contemporary environment where Bien could relax and feel inspired, especially since he was working from home.

UNCOVER YOUR COLOURS

For the living area, we drew inspiration from his trip to Baguio, where he bought a salakót—a hat made of natural woven materials. He wanted his space to be very light and neutral with some accent colours speckled in. I actually really love neutrals, but that doesn't mean they can't be warm and interesting! For an accent, purple pillows remind Bien of his mom's favourite colour.

SHOP TILL YOU DROP

We covered the old blue carpet using two 8 by 10-foot cream-coloured rugs with subtle patterns and textures. This change alone transformed the room and brightened up the space. Then, we picked out an oat-coloured sofa to continue with the creamy tones. This sofa has a versatile, timeless silhouette. The wood base adds some warmth and textural contrast. Two velvet poufs in the nook offer extra seating, which can easily be tucked under the table to save space.

BEFORE

188

MOCK IT UP

Creating a Pinterest board was the best way for me to communicate my ideas with Bien for his project.

BRING ON THE BALANCE

We removed the track lighting and added a large, sculptural woven pendant light to bring shape and fill the negative space in the room—colour is just one way to build visual interest. Then we layered and added contrast to the rest of the space with shades of green, plants, vintage pieces, natural materials, fixtures, and art.

WOW IT OUT

A raffia wall sconce doubles as a light fixture and as art on the walls in the eat-in nook. This look is achieved by stacking two plug-in sconces to create a striking architectural moment. I printed two 30 by 40-inch prints of mine and hung them side by side to create a focal point behind the sofa. I found a handwoven inabel throw blanket from Ilocos, Philippines. The traditional pattern is called kusikus, which is a circular pattern known for its dizzying appearance, believed to ward off bad vibes.

COLOURBLOCKED BEDROOM

Bien's bedroom didn't reflect his free-spirited, colour-loving personality. The previous layout had the bed awkwardly placed in front of the windows, leaving no room to hop into bed from either side. We drew inspiration from the desert, which is one of his favourite places to get away. The colour story was inspired by a desert artwork we found that has sandy terra-cotta colours with faded blue skies. Then we picked out a rounded headboard with an abstract, painterly pattern to be the focal point in the bedroom. A patterned headboard is an easy way to add personality and visual interest to a space. I decided to do a terra-cotta colour block on the walls with a thin strip of navy to add contrast and continue with the navy accents. The artworks from Minted help bring the space together. What a relief to know that Bien is resting his head each night in a bedroom worthy of his colourful character.

Bien's apartment is a testament to the fact that if you live in a plain box of a space, using paint blocking, limewashing, and sculptural lighting can add architectural elements. And if you hate your carpet, throw down some rugs to make the space feel as new as possible. He tells me he feels like he's in New York's West Village now.

PAINT IN COLOUR BLOCKS

A fun way to add colour into a space is to utilise different colours to add dimension and the illusion of depth to a small room. Paint the walls two tones, using a darker colour on the bottom to carry the space. Adding a thin 1-inch darker line will create even more depth. Here, the navy blue we chose ties in the walls with the headboard. The two paint tones, paired with a defined line, add the illusion of architectural details in a room that has none. This completely changed the visual weight of the room.

BEFORE

Break the grid: hang artworks that overlap the line to make things more interesting.

KIM'S KOREATOWN APARTMENT

OLD

Kim has been renting this one-bedroom apartment in Koreatown, Los Angeles, for over ten years. The rent is super affordable, which is something that's practically impossible to find in Los Angeles, so she plans on staying put for a while. Her bedroom was small and didn't have a good flow, and the bathroom wasn't functional for her daily regimen. But her living room was spacious with a faux fireplace that added an architectural element.

BRAND

Kim is a fantastic cook. Her signature dish is Hainan chicken rice, which happens to be one of my favourite foods in the world. She loves the outdoors and recently got into fencing, as well. Her favourite flower is sunflower, so my plan was to imbue its colours into her space.

NEW

Even though she's renting, we were able to make the apartment feel custom by using wallpaper, creating a DIY headboard, updating her bathroom, and adding bold colour to the living room.

PLUM & PERSIMMON BEDROOM

To create a better layout, we placed the bed in the middle of the room so that you can walk by both sides of the bed. This is also good for one's romantic fêng shui, as placing a bed in one corner sends the message that only one person will be getting into the bed. Taking inspiration from a boutique hotel I stayed in, we created a custom DIY headboard that spans the entire length of the wall the bed is on. The wallpaper print is inspired by vintage handloomed Baule ikat cloth from West Africa. When I saw this in a plum colour, I thought it was unique and added a bold pattern to a previously quiet space.

BEFORE

REENERGISED BATHROOM

The bathroom was desperate for attention. My first task was to update the countertop and sink, both of which were too high. Kim is a grown woman, but like a toddler in preschool she had to use a stool every night and morning to wash her face. I had a piece of quartz fabricated to fit a new copper undermount sink. Kim loved this lily pad wallpaper because it reminded her of a jacket her mom owned that had lilies on it. We painted the cabinet Behr "Royal Orchard" to match the wallpaper.

For the floors we used peel-and-stick tiles to cover up the old, hideous existing tiles. As a renter, you're certainly not doing any permanent tile work, but peel-and-stick tiles are an impermanent, reversible solution that can refresh the space to make it feel more like your own. I updated the medicine cabinet to a wood-framed option that lends some warmth and plays well off of the copper sink.

The walk-in shower needed to be updated as well. It had a grimy frosted shower door. And tiles that were in bad condition. I decided to reglaze the tiles back to a bright and shiny white that looked like new. Then I installed a glass shower door to allow light into the shower and make it feel more open. Kim said it now feels like a spa in there!

REGLAZING FOR THE WIN

If you're living in a home with dated, old, broken, or grimy tiles, reglazing the tiles can make all the difference. Hire a professional to reglaze your tiles, which keeps the existing tiles in place but makes them feel new without any demo work. Here's the fun part: the glazes come in all types of colours, so you can truly reimagine your space.

BEFORE

BUDGET-FRIENDLY KITCHEN

I am all about cheap and cheerful ways to update a space, and using peel-and-stick subway tiles for a kitchen backsplash is one of the best ways to change the vibe. No renovation required! Kim's old backsplash featured dated glass mosaic tiles. So, we picked simple white peel-and-stick subway tiles to brighten up the kitchen. We painted the island a teal blue to add some much-needed colour and contrast. Kim also wanted counter stools that were upholstered and had some back support, so we swapped out her old metal industrial stools.

BEFORE

SUNNY LIVING ROOM

Since one of Kim's favourite flowers is the sunflower, and she wanted a laid-back vibe for her living room, we painted over the grey walls and ceiling with a bright yellow (Valspar "Sunday Brunch"). We chose an orange, curved sofa to play with the warm tones and an armchair with rounded edges for a cosy vibe. The coffee and accent tables are also rounded, which creates a smooth flow around the space instead of running into sharp corners. Even the chandelier and table lamp have curvy designs to make it feel relaxed and airy. A neutral rug with graphic lines anchors the room. Instead of hanging the artworks above the mantel, we chose to lean them against the wall for a more casual look. The rust-colour print ties in with the colour of the sofa. Overlap artworks in different sizes to create variation in height. Mix in wood, woven textures (knits, throws, and pillows), and ceramics to add warmth to a space.

SEVEN WAYS TO UPDATE YOUR RENTAL

1. LIGHTING

Updating lights is probably my favourite way to accessorise a space and make it feel instantly elevated. And it can be quite easy. Most people think you need an electrician because it looks intimidating to change out a light, but I've taught all the people featured in this book how to do it. Here are some easy options.

PLUG-IN SCONCES: Typically, sconces require in-wall electrical wiring. It makes the space feel custom, but if you're renting, you're probably not going to be allowed to open up walls to put one in. It can be costly, too. That's where plug-in sconces do the trick.

SWAG LIGHTS: If you don't have any ceiling lights or simply want to add one to a room without using an electrician, a swag light is a great option. You can pair many cord kits with most pendant shapes and sizes, so the possibilities are endless.

2. PEEL-AND-STICK WALLPAPER, TILES, AND HOOKS

If your apartment has a backsplash in your kitchen that you're not excited about (or no backsplash at all), peel-and-stick wall tiles are your best friend. They are typically made of vinyl and are thicker than wallpaper. They come in different styles and can instantly change a kitchen without having to do any renovations. Similarly, removable wallpaper is another quick and easy way to add pattern to a space without having to paint. I also love using peel-and-stick hooks for hand towels.

3. LIGHT SWITCH PLATES

Many people overlook switch plates, but they are so underrated. We often touch them to turn them off and on, so why not give something you use daily a little update? I love brass switch plates from Legrand or Schoolhouse.

4. PAINT

The power of paint never fails to amaze me. Walls, cabinets, old furniture, you name it—give old spaces or things a new life with a fresh coat of paint.

5. HARDWARE FOR DOORS AND CABINETS

Another thing that you touch daily: doorknobs and handles. You'd be amazed by how easy it is to screw in a new knob or pull to give your cabinets or doors a quick update. Here are some of my favourite hardware companies: Emtek, Schoolhouse, and Rejuvenation.

6. WINDOW TREATMENTS

I am a firm believer in Roman shades. They are easy to install, so you can gently remove those vertical blinds, store them away in a closet or give them to your landlord. SelectBlinds.com has a lot of options.

7. FAUCETS

If you're not relatively handy yourself, hire a plumber or someone skilled to help you swap out your plumbing fixtures. Sometimes, changing the metal finish in your bathroom or kitchen plumbing fixtures can make a big impact on the space without doing a full remodel. Bringing in a new fixture can also help improve your water pressure if the existing one is old and clogged from years of use.

DAB-IT-YOURSELF
WALL-TO-WALL HEADBOARD

I once stayed at a boutique hotel where the bed's headboard spanned the entire wall. I thought that was a really neat way to add a bit of flair in a bedroom. It also makes the space feel more enclosed and allows the bed to be the focal point. And since finding the perfect headboard for your bed frame can be tricky, why not DIY your own? For a more custom look, I recommend creating a wall-to-wall headboard in your choice of fabric. You want the headboard to extend past the nightstands to frame the bed, becoming a strong focal point. Once the headboard is complete, simply sit it on the floor against a platform bed frame with the nightstands pushed up against it for support. Here are some easy steps to help guide you.

WHAT YOU'LL NEED

Tape measure

¼-inch-thick plywood, dimensions depend on the size of wall

Gorilla Tape

Foam (we used 1-inch-thick foam, but you can go thicker)

Scissors

1633 foam lock adhesive spray

Batting

Fabric

Staple gun

INSTRUCTIONS

STEP 1: Measure your wall, and then get ¼-inch-thick plywood to fit your desired length and height. You can get the boards cut into smaller pieces if needed. If you have a smaller vehicle, you'll definitely need to cut the boards for transporting home.

STEP 2: Lay the plywood pieces flat in one continuous line and use Gorilla Tape to tape the edge on both sides, from piece to piece, to create one long board. Lay the board on top of the foam and trim it to fit, leaving ¼ inch of foam around the edges.

STEP 3: Spray the foam lock adhesive on the back of the foam. Let it sit for 1 minute, then turn it over and adhere it to your plywood.

STEP 4: Spray the foam lock adhesive on top of the foam and let it sit for 1 minute before laying the batting over it. The batting should have a 5-inch allowance around the foam.

STEP 5: Now it's time to wrap your fabric around the board, over the batting. Use the staple gun to secure it to the back of the board.

HOLLY'S DENVER HOME

OLD

My aunt Holly bought a brand-new home in Denver, Colourado. It was a builder-grade home without much character and was still fairly empty inside. She hadn't prioritised making her house a home because she wasn't sure how long she'd stay in Denver, but fast-forward and it had been five years. It's similar to a lot of renters' mentalities; they think it's not a permanent place so they don't invest much into their space. Her home was inadvertent minimalism, to the max. While some immigrant stories I've shared deal with hoarding, my aunt went the complete opposite direction. I believe her empty space reflected the fact that she lost her spark after my uncle Joe passed away, and her dulled, hollow state was apparent in her home.

BRAND

Holly remains an important presence in my life because she always supported me whenever I needed it. She appreciates traditional and modern designs. One of her favourite colours is purple. And I remember she would always invite me into the kitchen to cook alongside her growing up. She loves using fresh herbs in her dishes. She once shared a meaningful story with me about the time when my family were refugees fleeing Vietnam and waiting to be sponsored to the United States: they were stationed on the island of Pulau Tengah in Malaysia for eight months, and she vividly remembers how life was so carefree and simple then. They lived by the ocean and didn't have any responsibilities. Food was provided daily. They built a community with other refugees and learned to sing and dance. I wanted to honor some of those memories and bring them into her new home.

NEW

My approach for Holly's house was to create a lot of wow moments because the home desperately needed them. We went with bold paint colours and wallpaper, and gave the windows some proper treatments. Her must-haves included a kitchen backsplash and a cosy, small lounge room that doubled as a mahjong room. I wanted to Dabify these spaces to inspire her and add some spark and verve back into her life.

STARTING OVER IN COLORADO

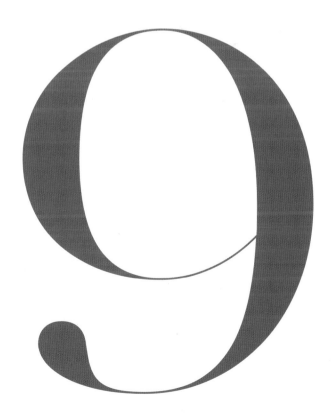

MOODY & MODERN BEDROOM

My aunt's favourite colour is purple, so I found a plum-coloured kilim rug to ground the bedroom. This woven, arched headboard, made from elephant grass from Ghana, paired with the Moroccan hand-braided raffia adds movement and makes for a beautiful, unique focal point. I swapped out the booby lamp for a sculptural brass baton pendant. During my forty-eight-hour blitz in which I styled Holly's space, I looked for items with texture, visual interest, and extra details any chance I could. For a fun accent, I chose green ceramic lamps with floral-pattern lampshades. The front of the nightstands are patterned in a Chinese geometric meander design.

Then I chose a deep, muted blue paint colour to add richness and cosiness. Painting all the walls and the ceiling the same colour is a great way to make a space even more bold and dramatic. Paint the baseboards and trims, too! We're so used to seeing everything white that people forget about the fifth wall, which is the ceiling.

BEFORE

215

ENGLISH-INSPIRED KITCHEN

So, here's a silly design idea: how about aluminum foil, straight from the roll, as a kitchen backsplash? Yes, that's a thing! While new builds are very generic, the plus side is that you can really put your own spin on things. We got rid of the foil and installed green zellige backsplash tiles that gave the kitchen more depth and variation. Since we didn't paint the cabinets, I used wallpaper to add texture and pattern to the space. The wallpaper design features herbs, which are very appropriate for the kitchen and reminiscent of my aunt's flavourful cooking. To warm up the space and add more contrast, we chose brass fixtures, gold hardware on the cabinets and doors, and woven stools. Painting the island Farrow & Ball "Duck Green" ties in with the tiles.

BEFORE

COOL & CONTEMPORARY LIVING ROOM

The living room is a large open-concept floor plan. To encourage gathering and ensure there isn't an empty void in the middle of your room, group furniture pieces in the centre. Anchor the space with a large area rug. We placed two 9 by 12-foot rugs next to each other to create one large 12 by 18-foot rug. Fill it up with multiple seating options like chairs, poufs, and a sectional to make it inviting. The bigger the room, the more you gotta fill it up! Painting the room a vivid blue colour also enlivens and defines the space from the adjacent rooms.

Since the paint colour on the walls is a cool tone, I balanced the blue with canary-yellow curtains.

Light fixtures are spread throughout the room at different heights to distribute light evenly and set ambience. Mixing two modern lights (the ceiling light and the floor lamp) with two vintage lamps brings out an eclectic vibe, which you can achieve by mixing old and new. This eclectic scene was ready for an equally eclectic gallery wall, which features a colourful collection of fiber art, paintings, and photo prints I made. Choosing a few art prints that echo both the blue paint colour on the walls and the yellow curtains ties the room together. The vintage red abstract painting on the adjacent wall throws everything a bit off-kilter in an unexpected way. Sometimes your art doesn't have to match your room and can serve as a bold statement piece.

My aunt Holly has always been like a second mom. She offered a lot of advice growing up and supported me in every way. In many ways, she was a big source of inspiration for me.

BEFORE

With a big space like this one, you want to pull your furniture pieces to the centre of the room to encourage gathering. Placing a coffee table, chairs, and other seating in the centre will ensure there isn't a large, empty void in the middle of your space. Use ottomans, accent chairs, and varying tables to play with your floor plan and fill the area.

SCALED-UP DINING ROOM

Inspiration for the dining room came from my aunt's specific memory of a time right before my family immigrated to the United States. They were in Malaysia, and she remembers it being relaxed and carefree, like it was a vacation. My aunt wanted this dining room to be completely white, so I chose blue Roman shades, which hint to the colours of the ocean and sky. I thought of the rust-orange chairs as rays of the sun. The accents in the artwork, the plants, and the other accessories add a tropical touch. I think it's important to give a nod to your past and appreciate the journey, while also embracing what's still to come up ahead.

To balance out the white walls, we used a 10 by 14-foot vintage Persian rug to fill up the space. The dining room is fairly large, and smaller furniture could feel off-scale in here. We chose a larger, appropriately sized dining table that seats eight. A pair of vintage island paintings tie the space together.

BEFORE

CURVY & CORAL MAHJONG ROOM

WHAT WOULD DAB DO?

DISCOVER YOUR MUST-HAVES

This room is one of the first open spaces you see when you enter the home, so I wanted it to be a vibrant and energetic space. My aunt Holly wanted this room to be a place where she could lounge or host mahjong sessions, or both. Growing up, our most prized possessions were our karaoke machine and a set of mahjong tiles that echo my heritage, my roots being in Hainan and Vietnam. If there's a soundtrack to my childhood, it would be the sounds of mahjong tiles clashing and all the aunties yelling, "Pong!" And also someone singing karaoke in the background. My family played mahjong almost every weekend. It was a way to connect, gossip, and release stress.

CREATE YOUR FLOOR PLAN

This is essentially a small living room or study that needed to double as a mahjong room. To encourage gathering and playing, ample seating through a sofa, accent chair, pouf, and mahjong table chairs dictates the flow of this floor plan. A small, round coffee table still fits the space when the foldable mahjong table is in use.

UNCOVER YOUR COLOURS

Finding a colour palette from specific art pieces and rugs is an excellent way to create a colour story for a space. I decided to go tone-on-tone and picked out a coral paint colour (Sherwin-Williams "Rojo Dust") for the entire room, along with matching curtains and rug.

SHOP TILL YOU DROP

I don't always know what the colour story is from the beginning, so I went hunting for an antique art deco Chinese rug. I knew the size was going to be 9 by 12 feet, and then I set the price limit to $1,500. These rugs are definitely a splurge for me, but they are so beautiful and, honestly, rare to find, especially at the price point I had set. But if there's any room that warrants an antique Chinese rug, it's a mahjong room. I stumbled upon this coral, floral beauty, and everything else flowed from there.

MOCK IT UP

I mocked up Aunt Holly's mahjong room in Photoshop, and it is almost identical to the final design. It just worked.

BRING ON THE BALANCE

With such a warm, dominant colour, balance was needed in a big way. If you look closely at the rug, you'll notice hints of blues. That's where I chose the opposing colour to make another statement. I found an Yves-Klein-Blue velvet curved sofa to activate this space. Yellow and white accent colours lighten it all up, keeping the design from being too coral-heavy.

WOW IT OUT

This whole room feels like a box of warm colour, creating an overwhelming wow moment the second you enter.

BEFORE

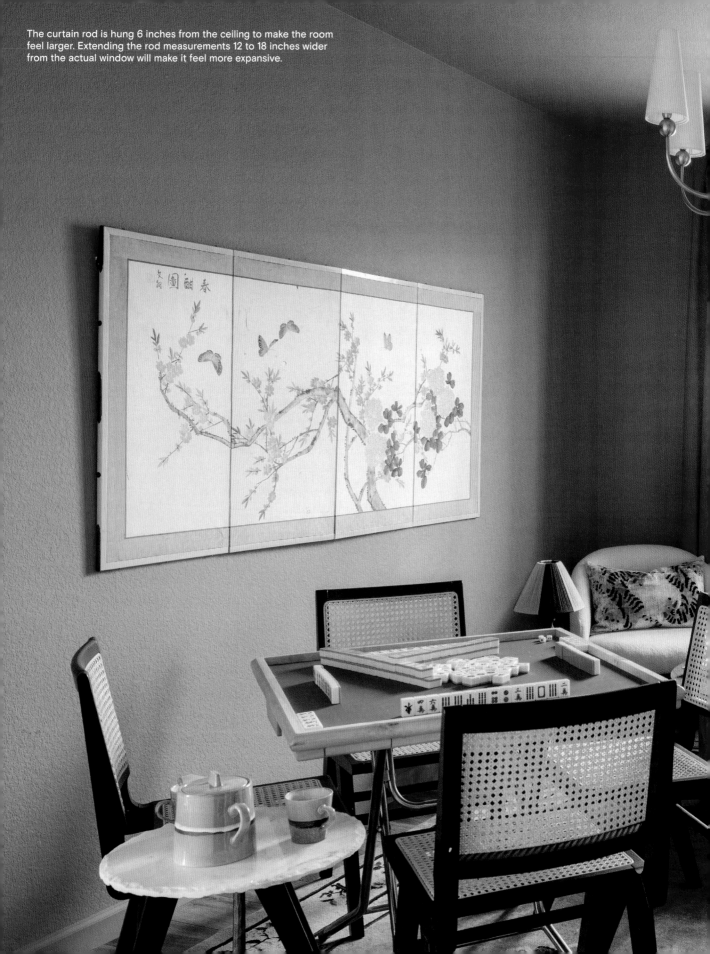

The curtain rod is hung 6 inches from the ceiling to make the room feel larger. Extending the rod measurements 12 to 18 inches wider from the actual window will make it feel more expansive.

HOW TO STYLE A COFFEE TABLE

Styling a coffee table is one of my favourite ways to teach people how to show their story! Think of this as an intimate window into some of your things and interests. It invites your guests to curiously go through the books, stories, and objects you've collected and proudly display. My foolproof way of styling a fun coffee table is to create a grid using books and trays. Once you have a grid you like, then you can fill in the pockets with round objects to break up the grid, like a vase with florals, candles, or catchall bowls and dishes. Here is your chance to share small items you've found from your travels or that were gifted by friends to show them that you value their gifts.

PLAY WITH SHAPES

The mahjong room is a celebration of curved and rounded edges and spheres. Pay attention to the details; sometimes intentionally leaning into a subtle theme is what can really make a design memorable.

DAB-IT-YOURSELF
HOW TO MAKE QUICK ART

When I traveled to Denver to redo my aunt Holly's house, I was worried we wouldn't be able to find enough art. Then she mentioned that she was given a free calendar and didn't know what to do with it, but it had beautiful art in it. So, here's another really affordable way to hang art, especially when you're in a pinch. I decided to cut out these beautiful Chinese watercolours from her calendar and frame them. They add so much colour and playfulness and are an affordable yet interesting solution for art in the home. The simple wooden frames are from Target. It's my go-to place for frames up to 16 by 20 inches.

WHAT YOU'LL NEED

Art from calendars, magazines, posters, books, etc.

Scissors

Tape measure

Frames

INSTRUCTIONS

STEP 1: Cut out the desired artwork.

STEP 2: Measure the artwork to make sure it fits into the frame you've chosen, then trim the excess.

STEP 3: Put the artwork into the frame. Now you're ready to hang!

OUR NEW ORLEANS COTTAGE

OLD

My husband, Ryan, and I spent a few years living together in Los Angeles, and when we got engaged, we decided to buy a cottage together in New Orleans. You can take the boy out of New Orleans, but you can't take New Orleans out of the boy. The vibrant energy of NOLA is intoxicating. There is something special in this laid-back, free-spirited, bohemian city that pulls people (like us!) back to it. This two-bedroom cottage in the Seventh Ward is a brand-new build. On one hand, I'm glad it didn't need any renovations. But on the other hand, it had zero character. Sometimes the brand new needs a touch of "old" to give it some soul. When we bought the home, it had all-white subway tiles, flat white walls, and nondescript white cabinets. Luckily the outside had blush-coloured siding, navy shutters, and a sage-green door for that touch of quintessential New Orleans charm. All we needed to do was bring that charm inside.

BRAND

Since my husband and I bought this home together, we wanted it to truly embody both of our styles. But blending another person's style with yours can take a bit of time to master. First, not only did we start a joint savings account, but we also created a joint Pinterest board where we shared interiors that we like. And then we talked about the common styles we like and absolutely dislike. Looking through his pins, Ryan loves antiques and things that have a lot of character and patina. While I'm a vintage vulture, my style tends to be more modern with cleaner lines. Luckily I love a lot of styles, and it's great to mix in his more intricate details with my sculptural pieces. When we decide on picking furniture, maybe I'll let him buy the furniture pieces while I select the colour, so it truly feels collaborative. It's the balance. He's the yin to my yang. That really adds an even more playful and interesting layer to the whole space.

NEW

The new vibe is to invite character and charm into this boring space. Our must-haves were adding focal points, wall treatments, colour, light fixtures, and, above all else, a cute backyard to entertain our New Orleans friends during Mardi Gras and all the fabulous festivals. Plus, Ryan loves going outside to soak in the humidity—it keeps the skin looking fresh and dewy!

A SOULFUL BRAND-NEW BUILD IN NEW ORLEANS

10

CURATED LIVING ROOM

As with most new builds, this living room was a bright, empty white box with infinite potential. It was fall when we got this house, so autumn colours were on our minds. We first chose a rich rust-coloured sofa and paired it with a lighter candy-yam accent wall (Behr "Shiny Kettle"). To balance the warm colours, we went with blue accent pillows, vases, an ottoman, and an antique Chinese rug with a blue border.

After a trip to Paris, my boo and I added dentil crown molding and wall trims inspired by the Parisian hotel we stayed at. We hired a contractor to help us install the molding we'd found at a local hardware store in all the rooms of the home. Voilà! It instantly gave the space more depth, character, and *élégance*. This new build now feels like it's been in New Orleans for a hundred years.

MIXED & MAXIMAL BREAKFAST NOOK

The sunny eating nook was inspired by our favourite turmeric gin-and-tonic cocktail. Our small cottage doesn't have a designated dining space, so we had the idea to squeeze a cosy area to eat in between the kitchen and living room. A small banquette against the wall gives us enough room to sit. We chose a round pedestal table because round tables are ideal for small spaces: they don't have space-hogging legs, and they're easier to navigate around. A small yellow-striped banquette was chosen to add pattern in the space since it sat directly across from the solid rust-coloured sectional.

The bistro table is also where I make cocktails. One of my favourite cocktails to make is my special gin and ginger–turmeric tonic. It has ginger, lemon, honey, and turmeric, so it's good for you with all the anti-inflammatory properties. A splash of gin gives it an extra botanical kick.

GIN AND GINGER-TURMERIC COCKTAIL

MAKES 1 COCKTAIL

1½ ounces gin (such as The Botanist) or your choice of spirit (mezcal is perfect as well)

3 ounces Ginger-Turmeric Tonic (recipe follows)

Fresh ginger, sliced, for garnish

Lemon slice, for garnish

In a cocktail shaker, combine the gin and the ginger-turmeric tonic with ice and give it a good shake. Strain the cocktail into a glass over fresh ice and garnish with the ginger and lemon slice. Enjoy!

GINGER-TURMERIC TONIC

MAKES TONIC FOR 2 COCKTAILS

2 teaspoons turmeric powder

1 (2-inch) knob ginger, peeled and grated

¼ teaspoon freshly ground black pepper, to activate the turmeric's beneficial properties

4 cups filtered water

¼ cup freshly squeezed lemon juice (from about 1 lemon)

2 tablespoons honey

In a small saucepan over medium-low heat, combine the turmeric, ginger, black pepper, and 2 cups of the water. Simmer for 10 minutes. Strain through a fine-mesh strainer into a heatproof container with a lid. Add the lemon juice, honey, and the remaining 2 cups water and stir to combine. Cover and refrigerate until chilled. Serve over ice.

CONTRASTED KITCHEN

Entertaining is my love language, so a kitchen is an important space to me. The kitchen was white on white, and it didn't reflect my vibe, but it was the perfect canvas to make it personal. I tried throwing a rug down to add interest, but even with the back door painted a sage green (Sherwin-Williams "Privilege Green"), colour alone was still not enough. I decided to change up some things without having to renovate. Updating the paint colour, faucets, and hardware is a great option for anyone who can't budget for remodeling but still wants a whole lot of impact.

I chose a deep, rich blue colour, Farrow & Ball "Inchyra Blue" (that, depending on the day, can read as navy or even teal) and contrasted it with "Champagne Bronze" finishes from Delta Faucet. Chrome is just not my thing for kitchens (or anywhere) if I don't have to use it. Gold, brass, or bronze finishes add so much more warmth.

Café curtains date back to the nineteenth century and were popular in Europe in—you guessed it—coffee shops or cafés. They're hung in the middle of the window instead of at the top, which gives privacy while allowing light in through the exposed upper part of the window. Here I cut two pieces of hemp Hmong fabrics with tassels and clipped them to a very inexpensive tension rod. Easy peasy. No screws needed. This touch adds softness to the kitchen.

I did a lot of research on painting cabinets and discovered New Orleans contractor Nathan Benoit, who specialises in refinishing cabinets using only industrial paint, which is more durable and dries faster, instead of enamel or acrylic (which are the only paint finishes I'd ever used prior). This process was a little more expensive. I ended up paying close to $6,000 for it, and this is a pretty small kitchen, too. But the outcome was outstanding, and the painted cabinets look like they came straight from the factory.

BEFORE

DRAMATIC BATHROOMS

Both of the bathrooms were the perfect blank canvases to add just a touch of drama. A really easy way to accentuate the height of a space is to hang your shower curtains close to the ceiling. The ceilings in our bathroom are 10 feet. It is quite difficult to find shower curtains longer than 72 inches, and typically they are only a single panel. You can treat this like it's a window. I found regular curtains that are 108 inches long. And if windows can have two panels, I don't see why showers can't. Don't forget to add a shower liner in combination with the curtain to repel water (which you can find easily with a quick online search). The rust accents in the towels and accessories play off the stripes on the curtain.

BEFORE

242

The wallpaper by Mind the Gap features Asian fruits and flowers. I used the pink accents in the wallpaper as a jumping-off point for accessories in the room, like the light fixture and vase.

A vintage Asian screen serves a creative use as a headboard. And by now, you're probably wondering why my bedding and pillowcases are usually white. Well, that's because I have acne-prone skin, and I use benzoyl peroxide daily, which will bleach any colourful dye. You have no idea how many sheets and shirts I've ruined in my lifetime. I also think white bedding is a clean foundation for creating contrast. Remember, it's about the yin and yang of light and dark colours or solids and patterns.

CHINOISERIE CHIC GUEST BEDROOM

I love designing guest bedrooms because you can flex your designs a bit to create a bolder space that you might be hesitant to do for your primary bedroom. After looking around the house and seeing mostly white, I wanted to give the bedroom a moody, floral, romantic feeling with vintage accents like chinoiserie, Asian art, and other handcrafted pieces. Since I'd been using many bright, vibrant colours in other spaces, I wanted to create a darker room. I picked out a navy blue/teal (Behr "Juniper Berries" in matte finish) for the walls, and painted the ceiling green (Behr "Royal Orchard") for a subtle but unexpected accent. For styling touches, I added in vintage throw pillows from Gujarat, India.

A good tip to remember is that you can paint baseboards, crown molding, and doors as well. People so often just stick with the walls when it comes to paint, but the trim, doors, and more are invisible lines we don't need to stop at. Painting outside the box is an approach that ends up giving your entire room a bolder, more elevated, and dramatic vibe.

Tip: Create a mirrored colour story by matching your rug to the ceiling colour, like this art deco Chinese green rug and the green ceiling.

FUNCTIONAL LAUNDRY ROOM

WHAT WOULD DAB DO?

DISCOVER YOUR MUST-HAVES

The goal was to take an empty closet and transform it into a lively and functional laundry room. This room also needed to have an organised storage system to decrease clutter and make the process of doing laundry more enjoyable. Cabinets and shelves were musts, along with a small stacked washer and dryer and a hanging rod for drying clothes. We also wanted to add a hidden outlet in the cabinets to charge our cordless vacuum and power drill.

CREATE YOUR FLOOR PLAN

With this being a tighter space with a small footprint, designing from the ground up was the plan. Incorporating vertical shelving and a stackable washer and dryer packs more functionality into the room without taking up a lot of space. Stacking the washer and dryer also allowed room for two cabinets to be installed. Always remember that you can maximise a small space by designing vertically.

UNCOVER YOUR COLOURS

I always like having a yellow room wherever I live, so I thought it would be a fun surprise to open up the closet and be greeted by this bright yellow for a little unexpectedness. We painted the entire space and the cabinets yellow. It feels like a ray of sunshine every time I open the doors. I encourage you to think of a colour that you identify with or a colour that inspires you. Use your signature colour throughout your life and your spaces!

SHOP TILL YOU DROP

Custom cabinets can be expensive and have a long lead time. For this small space, I looked for cabinets in stock at my local hardware store, and I found both a counter-height and tall cabinet. I bought them and had them painted and assembled quickly, so this is a great option for a fast turnaround.

MOCK IT UP

Remember that you can always draw your plans on paper. I freehand sketched the configuration of the shelves, cabinets, and washer and dryer.

BRING ON THE BALANCE

Bringing in woven elements like baskets softens the bright yellow space. Black accents add contrast, while pops of sage green cool down the room. I painted this watercolour and hung it above the counter cabinet to spice it up. Brass knobs bring out a tonal vibe in this sunny laundry room.

WOW IT OUT

The colour is the wow! Painting an entire closet yellow is a bold statement.

BEFORE

TINY & LIVELY BACKYARD PATIO

Our backyard is narrow, which makes designing a bit tricky. Because all New Orleans homes are raised, we decided to extend the deck all the way to the fence. We hired contractors to create this using tongue-and-groove wood flooring, along with a horizontal fence to elongate and widen the appearance of the narrow space. Once those practicalities were behind us, it was time to have a little fun with my favourite design feature—colour! I took inspiration from our cottage home, which has pink siding, green doors, and blue shutters. We chose a navy-blue wood stain (Behr "Atlantic" Semi-Transparent) for the floors and a chocolate wood stain (Behr "Chocolate" Semi-Transparent) for the fence. I love to entertain, even if it's just having a few close friends over for cocktails, so offering an outdoor space to socialise is great for Saints games.

BEFORE

DAB-IT-YOURSELF
HOW TO CREATE A GALLERY WALL

As you know by now, I am all about a gallery wall or a "galwall," as I like to call it. We all need a galwall. It will never go out of style.

Gallery walls date back to the 1600s in France and were called salon walls. And salons were essentially event spaces filled with artworks crammed on the walls from floor to ceiling. Artworks hung at eye level were deemed most important or influential by the exhibitors.

When choosing art for your gallery wall, you should have mostly medium to large artworks. If artworks are too small, they can look cluttered and messy. Here's my quick and easy way of doing a gallery wall.

WHAT YOU'LL NEED

Pencil

Nails

Hammer

Tape measure

Artworks of your choosing

STEP 1: First measure the wall where you want to hang your gallery of artworks.

STEP 2: Place all your artworks on the floor, creating columns within the measurements you took from the wall. Columns are helpful in creating a grid for your art. Figure out the best art placement and what looks best next to each other. Planning out the configuration of your pieces on the floor will give you a visual template for hanging them on your wall. Centre the artworks in each column as you lay them out on the floor. And sometimes you can have two smaller artworks in a column or one larger artwork to fill two columns. This will make your gallery wall more interesting.

STEP 3: Once you've figured out your desired layout, snap a photo for reference, and it's time to hang your artworks. You can just eyeball and hang everything. I usually like a 2- to 3-inch gap between artworks from top to bottom, while placing the larger pieces in the centre of the gallery. If you have an object below your gallery wall like a table or a sofa, leave about 8 to 10 inches of space from the top of your object to the bottom of the lowest artwork. If it helps, you can hang the lowest piece in your gallery configuration first.

A SOULFUL BRAND-NEW BUILD IN NEW ORLEANS

255

TELL YOUR COLOURFUL STORY

The act of intentionally decorating a space means surrounding yourself with things you've made, art given to you from friends, plants you've cultivated, vintage treasures you've found for a song, souvenirs from travels, and family heirlooms. When you sit in these spaces, you will be reminded that you are loved, you are worthy, and that you belong. And nobody can take that feeling away from you. That is the power of decorating. To decorate your space with your story and what makes you *you* is to celebrate your life.

If you don't know where to start, focus on your favourite colour. Look for a repeated theme in your life. Start a Pinterest board and pin photos of interiors that make you happy. After you've gathered your inspiration, see what commonality is found from photo to photo. Did you save a lot of rooms with green in them? Do each of these rooms have similar patterns? Are there a lot of artworks or bold wallpapers? Next, visit your local bookstore and purchase some interior design magazines. Tear out your favourite pages and tape them on the wall. This will give you an analog mood board of what vibe or style you gravitate toward. Once you've identified what calls to you most from these images, you can apply that to your own home.

Decorating is a lot of testing things out—it's like trying on clothes. Move your furniture around, test a paint colour on the wall, redecorate your shelves, and allow your space to grow with you. Focus on what items reflect you and add joy to your space.

The treasured things and colours you surround yourself with are your affirmations. And it's never too late to start new stories, new collections, and new traditions. Surrounding ourselves with these things will always provide an unwavering foundation as we navigate life through its joys and struggles. I hope you celebrate all that you are and let your home be your safe space that nurtures your well-being, energy, and creativity. No matter your space, you have the ability to tap into your personality to make your home uniquely yours and beautiful.

Old Brand New is not just about space, it's a personal journey. For me, writing this book meant coming to terms with my journey—all the good parts and the tough parts. It's about opening yourself up and realising that you deserve a beautiful and luxurious life. It's about owning your strengths, owning your struggles, and owning your space to let your creativity come to life. And after decorating all these spaces, I realised we share a common thread: we all have colourful stories. It's never too late to identify the colourful parts of you and bring them into your home.

THE TREASURED THINGS AND COLOURS YOU SURROUND YOURSELF WITH ARE YOUR AFFIRMATIONS.

RESOURCES

ART AND PRINTING / FRAMING

Art Works Fine Art Publishing (Los Angeles): FineArtPublishing.com

Artsy: Artsy.net

Artsper: Artsper.com

Avenue Art and Framing (New Orleans): AvenueArtAndFraming.com

Beth Schiffer Fine Art Printing (New York City): BethSchiffer.com

Framebridge: Framebridge.com

Lost Art Salon: LostArtSalon.com

minted.: Minted.com

Old Brand New Shop: Shop.OldBrandNew.com

Simply Framed: SimplyFramed.com

Society6: Society6.com

Tappan: TappanCollective.com

BOOKS FOR COLOUR INSPIRATION

A Dictionary of Colour Combinations (Seigensha)

Beige Is Not a Colour: The Full-Spectrum World of Carlos Mota by Carlos Mota (Vendome Press)

Ellsworth Kelly by Tricia Y. Paik (Phaidon)

Patterns of India: A Journey Through Colours, Textiles, and the Vibrancy of Rajasthan by Christine Chitnis (Clarkson Potter)

Interaction of Colour by Josef Albers (Yale University Press)

The Secret Lives of Colour by Kassia St. Clair (Penguin Books)

Textiles of Southeast Asia: Tradition, Trade and Transformation by Robyn Maxwell (Periplus Editions)

BRICK-AND-MORTAR HOME DECOR

Beam (Brooklyn): BeamBK.com

Dyphor New York: DyphorShop.com

Jayson Home (Chicago): JaysonHome.com

Lawson-Fenning (Los Angeles): LawsonFenning.com

Modern Nomad (Denver): ModernNomadDenver.com

Sunday Shop (New Orleans): SundayShop.co

FURNITURE

Burke Decor: BurkeDecor.com

Castlery: Castlery.com/us

HD Buttercup: HDButtercup.com

Interior Define: InteriorDefine.com

Jonathan Adler: JonathanAdler.com

Kathy Kuo Home: KathyKuoHome.com

One Kings Lane: OneKingsLane.com

Soho Home: SohoHome.com/us

Valyou: ValyouFurniture.com

HOME DECOR

Goodee: GoodeeWorld.com

HKliving: HKLiving.com

Jungalow: Jungalow.com

Smallable: Smallable.com

Vermillion: VermillionLifestyle.com

Whitney J Decor: WhitneyJDecor.com

LIGHTING

Honoré: HonoreDeco.com

Mitzi: Mitzi.com

Sazerac Stitches: SazeracStitches.com

PAINT

Behr: Behr.com

Clare: Clare.com

Farrow & Ball: Farrow-Ball.com

Portola Paints & Glazes: PortolaPaints.com

Sherwin-Williams: Sherwin
-Williams.com

Sydney Harbour Paint Company:
SHPCompany.com

PLANTS AND FLORALS

Airluma: ShopAirluma.com

Antigua Floral: AntiguaFloral.com

Bia Blooms: BiaBlooms.com

Folia: FoliaCollective.com

Plant Therapy: PlantTherapy.com

PlantVine: PlantVine.com

Sacred Thistle: SacredThistle.com

San Gabriel Nursery & Florist:
SGNursery.com

Whit Hazen: WhitHazen.com

RUGS AND TEXTILES

Bolé Road Textiles:
BoleRoadTextiles.com

Eva Sonaike: EvaSonaike.com

Linoto: Linoto.com

Nordic Knots: NordicKnots.com

Revival: RevivalRugs.com

Rug Source: RugSource.com

SelectBlinds: SelectBlinds.com

The Citizenry: The-Citizenry.com

Water Air Industry:
WaterAirIndustry.com

Xasmin Interiors: XasminInteriors
.com

xN Studio: xNStudio.com

TILES

clé: CleTile.com

concrete collaborative: Concrete
-Collaborative.com

Fireclay Tile: FireclayTile.com

Riad Tile: RiadTile.com

TileBar: TileBar.com

Wonder Design:
WonderDesignStone.com

Zia Tile: ZiaTile.com

VINTAGE

1stDibs: 1stDibs.com

Badlands Vintage: @Badlands
.Vintage

Bonita Interiors: @BonitaInteriors

Casa Victoria: CasaVictoriaLA.com

Chairish: Chairish.com

DeKor: DeKorLiving.com

Dobbin Street Vintage Co-op:
DobbinStCoop.com

Garage Vintage (Denver):
GarageVintage.Weebly.com

The Luxe Lust Life:
@TheLuxeLustLife

Merchant House: @Merchant
_House.Co

Pasadena Antique Center and
Annex: PasadenaAntiqueCenter
.com

Pop Up Home: PopUpHome.com

Sunbeam Vintage:
SunbeamVintage.com

WALLPAPER

Cole & Son: Cole-and-Son.com

Hygge & West: HyggeAndWest
.com

Milton & King: MiltonAndKing
.com

RoomMates: RoomMatesDecor
.com

Tempaper: Tempaper.com

Wallpapers To Go:
WallpapersToGo.com

Walls Republic: WallsRepublic.com

Wallshoppe: Wallshoppe.com

SOURCES

PAGE 20: GREEN KITCHEN
Paint: Behr "Royal Orchard." Antique terra-cotta Mediterranean vase with waxflowers. Thai khantoke (tray). Vintage Copco tea kettle. Art: Justina Blakeney. Wow Design "Fez Emerald" tiles. Japanese Tokusa dinnerware. Delta Faucet. Florals: Dephiniums. Plant: Begonia maculata.

PAGE 24: DINING ROOM
Antique Bobbin corner chair. Wallpaper: Wallsrepublic "Tropical." Art: Dabito. Banquette: Ballard Designs in Sunbrella fabric. Hmong pillows. Dining table: Noir "Julia." Chandelier: Mitzi x Dabito "Hikari." Roman shades: SelectBlinds.

PAGE 28: LIVING ROOM
Paint: Behr "Night Blooming Jasmine." Antique Chinese art deco rug. Vintage wooden Indian chowki (stool). Purple mushroom pouf. Art: Dabito. Plant: Ficus Audrey. Chandelier: Jonathan Adler "Caracas." Vintage Rosenthal Netter vase. Pillows: Bolé Road Textiles. Plug-in sconces: Mitzi "Riley."

PAGE 39: HALLWAY
Paint: Farrow & Ball: "Faded Terracotta." Runner: Revival "Dahl." Plants: Ficus Audrey (left) and Dracaena (centre). Plant stand: Schoolhouse. Art: Bethania Lima, Nancy Ramirez.

PAGE 40: OFFICE/GUEST ROOM
Wallpaper: Milton & King "Travelers." Antique art deco Chinese rug. Plant: Kentia Palm. Bookcase: Room & Board. Coffee table: Schoolhouse.

PAGE 45: GREEN BATHROOM
Paint: Behr "Forest Edge." Plants: Lacy tree philodendron, monstera, Chinese money plant. Mirror: Rejuvenation. Sconce: Sazerac Stitches. Villa Lagoon Tile "Spark." Delta Faucets.

PAGE 48: PRIMARY BEDROOM & EN SUITE BATHROOM
Bedroom—Paint: Behr "Night Blooming Jasmine." Blanket: Jungalow. Nightstand: Jonathan Adler. Table lamp: Soho Home. Florals: Dahlias. Pendant: Anthropologie "Eloise." Bathroom—Paint: Behr "Golden Aura." Wallpaper: Cole & Sons "Alicatado." Tiles: Fireclay "Sea Glass" (floor), Riad Zellige Tiles "Natural White." Terrazzo tile: Concrete Collaborative.

PAGE 59: CINNAMON BATHROOM
Tiles: Marazzi "Zellige Carallo."

PAGE 60: OFFICE
Paint—Wall: Farrow & Ball "Eating Room Red." Ceiling: Farrow & Ball "Arsenic." Dining table: Castlery. Pendant light: Mitzi x Dabito "Sodsai."

PAGE 63: OUTDOOR OASIS
Plants: Bird of paradise and Boston fern.

PAGE 65: LAUNDRY ROOM
Paint: Behr "Rice Curry" (doors).

PAGE 74: LIVING ROOM
Chairs: Sun at Six "Plume."

PAGE 79: BEDROOM
Wallpaper: Tempaper. Bed: Novogratz. Bedding: The Company Store. Art: Amber Textiles.

PAGE 85: LIVING ROOM
Vintage Moroccan rug. Furniture: Castlery. Art: Mai Trung Thu, Otomi. Plant: Dracaena.

PAGE 88: MOM'S BEDROOM
Paint: Farrow & Ball "Rangwali." Vintage Ziegler rug. Antique ginger jar lamps. Tibetan tiger throw. Ikat pillows. John Derian peony plates.

PAGE 94: ELAINE'S BEDROOM
Wallpaper: Scott Living "Westport Coffee Geometric." Vintage 1970s nightstand. Gujarati pillows. Plant: Variegated Ficus altissima.

PAGE 99: KAILEY'S BEDROOM
Paint: Sherwin-Williams "Tricorn Black." Wallpaper: York Wallcoverings "Sketchbook." Malawi chair. Gujarati pillows and blanket.

PAGE 106: SOPHIA'S LIVING ROOM
Paint: Behr "Night Blooming Jasmine." Furniture: AllModern. Vintage Moroccan runner. Plant: Ficus binnendijkii.

PAGE 113: ENTRYWAY
Paint: Behr "Royal Orchard."

PAGE 114: BEDROOM
Wallpaper: Wallsrepublic "Saffron Tropical." Plant: Rubber tree plant.

PAGE 121: LIVING ROOM
Paint: Sherwin-Williams "Kilkenny" (door), Sherwin-Williams "Snowbound" (walls). Vintage Van Dyver-Witt sofa. Mali mud cloth. Kilim pillows. Jute rugs. Lights: Sazerac Stitches. Senufo stool. Tonga baskets.

PAGE 125: DINING ROOM
Paint: Farrow & Ball "Babouche." Art: Leroy Miranda Jr. chandelier: Jonathan Adler "Caracas." Live edge dining table.

PAGE 129: SUNROOM
Paint: Valspar "Royal Navy." Pillows: xN Studio. Vintage Moroccan rug. Juju hat. Plant: Yucca.

PAGE 130: CORNER DESK
Vintage peacock mirror. Plants: Dracaena, Chinese fan palm. Senufo stools.

PAGE 133: BEDROOM
Wallpaper: Justina Blakeney. Peruvian frazada (blanket) and pillows. Brutalist nightstands.

PAGE 134: BATHROOM
Paint: Sherwin-Williams "Surf Green." Tiles: Villa Lagoon Tile "Cubes." Art: SheShe. Vintage Moroccan runner.

PAGE 137: BEDROOM
(left) Paint: Sherwin-Williams "Parisian Patina." Vintage nemadji pottery vase. Antique campaign dresser. (opposite) Inabel throw blanket from Ilocos, Philippines. Art: Marc Reagen.

PAGE 138: MUDROOM
Paint: Sherwin-Williams "Dishy Coral." Plants: Yew tree, Chinese fan palm. Real Good chair. Vintage Moroccan rug.

PAGE 141: CURB APPEAL
Paint: Sherwin-Williams "Cadence." Plants: ferns, philodendrons, ginger plants, and Kentia palm.

PAGE 142: BACKYARD
Paint: Sherwin-Williams "Adriatic Sea," "In the Navy," and "Black" wood stain. Plants: Boston fern. Kilim pillows.

PAGE 157: LIVING ROOM
Paint: Behr "Night Blooming Jasmine."

PAGE 160: DINING ROOM
Paint: Behr "Terra Cotta Clay."

PAGE 163: BATHROOM
Paint: Behr "Pine Brook."

PAGE 166: BEDROOM
Paint: Farrow & Ball "Setting Plaster." Beni Ourain Moroccan rug. Bedding: Parachute.

PAGE 168: NURSERY
Wallpaper: York Wallcoverings "Sprig & Heron." Vintage Moroccan rug.

PAGE 176: KITCHENETTE
Paint: Behr "Fig Tree" (cabinets), Behr "Sage Brush" (wall). Tiles designed by Dabito with Saba Tiles.

PAGE 181: LIVING SPACE & BEDROOM
Pillows: Kelly Wearstler, Justina Blakeney, Bolé Road Textiles. Vintage Moroccan rug. Light: Dabito x Mitzi "Liwa."

PAGE 185: BATHROOM
Paint: Behr "Lamplit."

PAGE 188: LIVING ROOM
Paint: Portola "Mission" lime wash (living room), Portola "Korine" lime wash (accent wall nook). Charlotte Perriand rio coffee table. Light pendant from Dyphor NYC. Plant: Ficus Audrey. Thai pillows. Raffia plug-in sconces. Art by Dabito.

PAGE 195: BEDROOM
Paint: Behr "Canyon Dusk" and "Nocturne Blue." Art: Minted. Cane pendant. Vintage 1950s Polynesian wood art.

PAGE 201: BEDROOM
Wallpaper: Wallshoppe "Madison Stripe." Vintage Hmong pillows.

PAGE 202: BATHROOM
Paint: Behr "Royal Orchard." Wallpaper: Roommates "Lily Pad."

PAGE 205: KITCHEN
Paint: Behr "Echo Park." Tsukiusagi kettle.

PAGE 206: LIVING ROOM
Paint: Valspar "Sunday Brunch." Hmong textiles. Plant: Ficus Audrey.

PAGE 215: HOLLY'S BEDROOM
Paint: Farrow & Ball "De Nimes." Table lamps: HK Living. Raffia mirror from Morocco. Headboard made from elephant grass in Ghana. Baton chandelier. Naga pillow. Custom Thai fabric. Flat-woven Kilim rug.

PAGE 216: KITCHEN
Paint: Farrow & Ball "Duck Green." Green zellige tiles.

PAGE 219: LIVING ROOM
Paint: Farrow & Ball "St Giles Blue." Flower: Gladiolus.

PAGE 222: DINING ROOM
Antique Dorokhsh Persian rug.

PAGE 225: MAHJONG ROOM
Paint: Sherwin-Williams "Rojo Dust." Tiger ikat pillow. Vintage maneki-neko cat. Antique art deco Chinese rug.

PAGE 235: LIVING ROOM
Paint: Behr "Shiny Kettle" (accent wall) and Sherwin-Williams "Privilege Green" (door). Antique art deco Chinese rug. Vase art: Anna Koeferl. Gujarati pillows. Hmong window treatment. Kantha throw. Furnishing from Crate & Barrel.

PAGE 241: KITCHEN
Paint: Farrow & Ball "Inchyra Blue."

PAGE 242: BATHROOMS
Wallpaper: Morris & Co "Fruit" and Mind the Gap "Asian Fruits and Flowers." Dusen Dusen striped robe. Hamsa hooks. Sconce: M Clément Studio.

PAGE 249: BEDROOM
Paint: Behr "Juniper Berries." Vintage Paul Mayen dome lamps. Gujarati pillows. Antique chinoiserie screen.

PAGE 250: LAUNDRY ROOM
Paint: Behr "Saffron Strands."

PAGE 253: PATIO
Paint: Behr "Chocolate" semitransparent wood stain (fence) and Behr "Atlantic" semitransparent wood stain. Sunbrella outdoor fabrics.

ACKNOWLEDGEMENTS

First and foremost, this book wouldn't exist without the enormous support and encouragement of my editor, Dervla Kelly, and the Ten Speed team. Thank you for seeing me and honoring my creative vision. I'm so grateful to be given this once-in-a-lifetime opportunity to share my story with the world.

My boo, aka favourite CLIENT, Ryan. Your approach to more functional living has pushed me to be a better designer. I'm lucky I found someone who loves decorating just as much as I do. From that magical moment when we met in Montauk until now, it's been a fabulous ride, and I'm looking forward to more colourful fights over sofas together.

I am grateful to my family. My mom, Kiu; sister, Elaine; aunt, Holly; and niece, Kailey, for keeping me grounded. I love you all so much.

Bien, Kim, Sophia and Rana, Anna and Ryan, thank you for inviting us into your intimate homes, sharing your stories, and showing us that it's never too late to live a luxurious life.

Lots of love to my work wife, Justina. You are a gifted visionaire. Your guidance in helping me with our (book) baby has been instrumental. Excited for our next adventure!

Shout-out to my friend Jen Li for your early help with getting my words and thoughts together.

I am super thankful for Kelli Kehler, my twin Aries flame, for sharpening this book and helping me make all these rooms sound as beautiful as I worked to make them.

Thank you to all my readers and vintage vultures who have been cheering me on from day one. You have been a vital part of my creative journey.

And to those who just discovered me, I hope this book inspires you to have fun celebrating *you* in your home. Make your spaces sing, because your home is the sound—er, karaoke—track to your life! You can't keep me from a karaoke reference!

ABOUT DABITO

Dabito is a designer, artist, photographer, and passionate vintage hunter. His use of bold colour and eclectic maximalism has cemented him as an always refreshing and ever-evolving influence in the world of interior design. Since 2010, his studio and blog, Old Brand New, amassed a devoted following across multiple platforms and has been recognised by *Better Homes & Gardens*, the *New York Times*, *Architectural Digest,* and *House Beautiful*. Dabito's guiding design philosophy is that everyone can harness the power of colour and meaningful objects to tell a moving and personal story in the home. He splits his time between Los Angeles and New Orleans with his husband, Ryan, and their fur babies, Luigi, Sterling, and Verbena.

This edition published in 2023 by Hardie Grant Books, an imprint of Hardie Grant Publishing, by arrangement with Ten Speed Press, an imprint of Random House, a division of Penguin Random House LLC.

Hardie Grant Books (Melbourne)
Wurundjeri Country
Building 1, 658 Church Street
Richmond, Victoria 3121

Hardie Grant Books (London)
5th & 6th Floors
52–54 Southwark Street
London SE1 1UN

hardiegrant.com/books

A catalogue record for this book is available from the National Library of Australia

Old Brand New
ISBN 978 1 76145 032 7

10 9 8 7 6 5 4 3 2 1

Publisher: Michael Harry
Acquiring editor: Dervla Kelly
Production editor: Bridget Sweet
Designer: Lizzie Allen
Production designer: Faith Hague
Production manager: Jane Chinn, Todd Rechner
Copyeditor: Michelle Hubner
Proofreader: Kathy Brock

Colour reproduction by Splitting Image Colour Studio
Printed in China by Leo Paper Products LTD.

The paper this book is printed on is from FSC®-certified forests and other sources. FSC® promotes environmentally responsible, socially beneficial and economically viable management of the world's forests.